A PLUME BOOK

MENDING THE BROKEN BOND

DR. FRANK LAWLIS is a renowned psychologist, researcher, and counselor with more than thirty-five years' experience working with families. He is the cofounder of the Lawlis and Peavey Centers for Psychoneurological Change and was named a fellow by the American Psychological Association. Dr. Lawlis is board certified in both clinical and counseling psychology by the American Board of Professional Psychology, and he is also the chief content adviser for the *Dr. Phil* show. His published works include *The ADD Answer*, *The IQ Answer*, and *The Stress Answer*. He lives in Sanger, Texas.

Also by Frank Lawlis

The ADD Answer

The IQ Answer

The Stress Answer

MENDING THE BROKEN BOND

The 90-Day Answer
to Repairing Your
Relationship
with Your Child

DR. FRANK LAWLIS

A PLUME BOOK

PLUME
Published by the Penguin Group
Penguin Group (USA) Inc., 375 Hudson Street, New York, New York 10014, U.S.A. •
Penguin Group (Canada), 90 Eglinton Avenue East, Suite 700, Toronto, Ontario, Canada
M4P 2Y3 (a division of Pearson Penguin Canada Inc.) • Penguin Books Ltd., 80 Strand,
London WC2R 0RL, England • Penguin Ireland, 25 St. Stephen's Green, Dublin 2,
Ireland (a division of Penguin Books Ltd.) • Penguin Group (Australia), 250 Camberwell
Road, Camberwell, Victoria 3124, Australia (a division of Pearson Australia Group Pty.
Ltd.) • Penguin Books India Pvt. Ltd., 11 Community Centre, Panchsheel Park, New
Delhi – 110 017, India • Penguin Group (NZ), 67 Apollo Drive, Rosedale, North Shore
0632, New Zealand (a division of Pearson New Zealand Ltd.) • Penguin Books (South
Africa) (Pty.) Ltd., 24 Sturdee Avenue, Rosebank, Johannesburg 2196, South Africa

Penguin Books Ltd., Registered Offices: 80 Strand, London WC2R 0RL, England

Published by Plume, a member of Penguin Group (USA) Inc. Previously published in a
Viking edition.

First Plume Printing, September 2008
10 9 8 7 6 5 4 3 2 1

Illustration on page 80 by Laura Maestro

Ⓟ REGISTERED TRADEMARK—MARCA REGISTRADA

The Library of Congress has catalogued the Viking edition as follows:

Lawlis, Frank.
   Mending the broken bond : the 90-day answer to developing a loving relationship with
your child / Frank Lawlis.
      p. cm.
   Includes bibliographical references and index.
   ISBN 978-0-670-01834-5 (hc.)
   ISBN 978-0-452-28988-8 (pbk.)
 1. Parenting. 2. Parent and child. 3. Child rearing. I. Title.
   HQ769.L3154 2007
   649'.154—dc22   2007019556

Printed in the United States of America
Set in Sabon
Original hardcover design by Victoria Hartman

This book is dedicated to Susan,
my wife and the light of my life,
who taught me the healing power of love.

Acknowledgments

In all creative projects there are many people who contribute to the final result, but this book is special to me because it came from a relationship I discovered as love. Granted, I have gone through life as an academic, thinking I knew what love was all about, but it took me more than sixty years to see the true wonder of it. The person who took me by the hand and became my soul mate in this world of paradise is my wife, Susan Faye Franks.

Susan was my student more than twenty years ago, and I was intrigued with her intelligence and clever disposition, and probably a little distracted by her beauty as well, if truth be told. As the years rolled past we were in contact with each other for research design consultation as well as for discussions with our mutual friend Dr. Joel Butler. Fast forward to the Katrina disaster and her activities in that ordeal as well as further meetings on new approaches to mental problems. The spark that must have been there for years caught the wind of passion. We fell in love.

My life has been filled with this healing power of love, and within that mission this book was created. I am constantly amazed at how my life has been transformed with her support and creative intelligence. I can only hope that the reader will be able to feel the energy of this love in relation to the ultimate hope—for the world to experience what love is.

I could not write a book without acknowledging one of my best friends, Dr. Phil McGraw, who continues to support my work on his television show and in our lives. We have built a trusting bond over thirty years of mutual respect that is rare on this earth. We have walked many miles together in a mission of making things happen that have never happened before. And it is very likely that he is the smartest man I know.

My colleagues and best cheering section are Jan Miller and Shannon Miser-Marven. Besides being the best literary agents in the world, they have become friends whose purpose, they allege, is to enable me to publish my books worldwide. They have been led to believe that I am smart and truly believe I have the answers to the mysteries of the universe. Even though this belief is misguided, my relationship with them is extremely important to me.

Wes Smith has been my writing consultant for years and he brings life into my words. I believe that the man can make a phone book read like *A Tale of Two Cities*. His amazing talent has certainly been critical to whatever success I have had writing my truth and having someone actually understand me.

Several readers have helped form the result from their perspectives. All of them are geniuses in my view and have graciously added to my knowledge and supported some conclusions that might be on the edge with tremendous insight. They are Dr. John Chirman, professor at Harvard University, and Dr. Ann Miller, director of pastoral services at Cook Children's Medical Center.

Contents

Preface

I have seen thousands of children for one reason or another in forty years of working with kids. Regardless of how much professional training I have had in recognizing psychopathology and adjustment issues, I have discovered that most problems rest with inadequate skills to develop a loving relationship with someone else. I might add that this disturbance in developing loving bonds also explains most problems with adults as well.

I entered the field of psychology to help people, as most individuals clearly communicate with the application; however, when I entered the classrooms, that *help* word was quickly translated into diagnosis and therapy. Psychology does not pretend to deal with the indefinable and unreliable features of the human psyche or else it becomes an art and not a science. Those in the profession of psychology prefer the discipline to be considered alongside medicine as a healing science, and discourage anyone from even discussing the soft fringes of human experience. Each dynamic or behavior has to be reduced to measurable and researchable units. For example, there was huge relief when even the personal experience of pain could be calculated in subjective units of discomfort (SUDs) and could be brought to a linear measurement.

You could probably understand my dismay and frustration when I was given a textbook on human development on the first day of graduate school that consisted of children's responses to environmental stimuli as its entire content, as if the child's behavior had been reduced to that of a rat. This level of understanding children continued throughout my training and still exists today.

There's clearly a disinterest in teaching a child to love and to be loved although this primary issue is at the heart of the problem for nearly every child I have ever seen. For the great majority of referrals, the performances or intelligences required in school or as part of their participation in family or social life bring them to my door.

Where have we gone in our society or even in our world that we downgrade this critical concern that lays the grid for all of human conditions? We worry about competition from other countries in terms of knowledge and numbers of PhDs. Yet what makes a country successful and builds its resistance to invasion but love and loyalty toward it? The mark of a great nation is its success in providing its citizens with an abundance of happiness and success. How can we achieve this without the basic elements of bonding in relationships? Our religions speak to this priority.

As I have perused the literature on guidance with children in their quests for learning, I am struck with the fact that very little has been said about the compassion of the child and the need for love as part of the therapeutic process. Everyone seems to be developing computer and online instruction on how to make kids smarter or more competent in some skill, but what about the most important aspect: the love capacity. It will not be whether or not he or she remembers what πr^2 is or the past tense form of *to be* when the challenges of intimacy and bonding with another person arise. We have no classes in school that discuss how to love another person, especially a child in our care. Yet what will be the primary value that will be the guiding light when they face the evils and temptations of the world? How will they feel without the substance love offers them when they feel lonely and desperate, which they surely will?

The specific areas of the brain that are responsible for reading signals and communicating with other humans are being denied the stimulation they need to develop. And for most of these functions, there is a window of maximum benefit. Once time has passed in the developmental evolution of the child's brain, learning becomes more difficult.

The training and administration of love is an investment and it is never a losing proposition. This is the most basic ingredient of healing I know, and every child deserves to have the most unconditional love he or she can receive. We all do. This book is a step into that arena and I hope it will make a difference in the world of all children.

My interest in helping people usually centers around children and their problems in growing up. I am alarmed in this generation of care that there is so little attention paid to the love and compassion needed by these children as they go through some of the most challenging times of their lives. They are faced with some horrible ordeals in adapting to the expectations of the world while dealing with crises such as learning disabilities, family conflicts, bullying, and a huge set of other physical and developmental imbalances. There is a huge overlay of stress and psychological strain accompanying any transition.

I have a very wise and highly successful friend who has worked with people all her life (edging past eighty years as of this printing) and her comment was that in every case she knew, those who were raised in a home without affection and love were the hardest core. In her words, "they came from a dry hole of assurance that they were loved or could be lovable." Love was the major ingredient that created positive change. Interestingly, it was the learning of love for others that came first. With these observations in mind, I see that with all of our advances in health care, the only thing parents are usually offered is a pill to remedy their problems with their children.

The psychiatric community has insisted on lowering the age for diagnoses such as bipolar and depression disorders with the administration of medications that have little or no clinical evidence of effects or side effects. Mental health groups have started diagnosing attention deficit disorder at a 67 percent error rate in order to categorize some behavior for medical intervention rather than using more long-term approaches that would require change and confrontation.

In a great majority of cases I have seen and consulted on, although children might have these other problems, the most significant problem began with a lack of training in the art of loving themselves and others. By missing out on this critical part of development, I have noticed that the children have some intuition that they are missing a vital part of their heritage—their hearts.

Mending the Broken Bond

1

Understanding the Bonds of Love

Johanna and Frank came into the clinic in a last desperate effort to find some way to manage their misbehaving ten-year-old, Frank Jr. Their complaints were typical. Although they gave him everything he wanted, it was never enough. Their son yelled in anger and complained that his older sister got more attention and respect. But he could be very charming at times, especially when he wanted something—only to then fly into a rage without provocation.

This kind of behavior can seem like simple lack of parental control at first impression. But such hostility also can be a plea for love and for closer family bonds. That was the case with Frank Jr. By simply giving in to his demands, his parents were sending a message that the boy perceived as: "We don't like you and we know it and feel ashamed, so we will pay you off with presents."

How do I know this? Because Frank Jr. told me. He was devastated every time they gave in. He felt that he had a huge burden to bear because his name was "Jr." He said he knew he could never live up to expectations, so why bother trying? He'd developed the view that his older sister, Angela, was the favored child; she was the *nice* one, the good kid who always did the right thing. Under strains like these, the bond he had once had with his parents had snapped and they were at the end of their rope.

Frank Jr. and his parents learned how to develop a bond of love following the methods I will describe in this book. This is not to say that he became the model child, but he did learn to trust that his parents loved him and that they were always acting out of love and concern. For him, this was a big step in the right direction.

Children who lash out can take parents to the edge. There are plenty of professionals and nonprofessionals willing to tag them with labels and drug them with medications to give parents relief. But at least 90 percent of these "worst cases" are actually just normal kids desperately looking for love and understanding. Rarely do I see parents who do not love their children. Most will fight to the grave for them, but many parents are in desperate need of ways to develop bonds of love and understanding with their children.

Do you sometimes feel that your children treat you more like a servant than a respected parent? Do your kids feel entitled to things that you consider privileges? Do they get angrier and unhappier even as you give them more and more? Does your relationship with your children seem to be in a downward spiral?

Has the fun gone out of parenthood? Do you fear that you and your children will never form a bond?

You are not alone in such feelings. Thousands of parents have shared these and other frustrations with me in my many years as a family counselor. I understand how it hurts parents to give and give of themselves and get nothing but disrespect and rebellion in return.

In the survey of 20,000 parents conducted for Dr. Phil McGraw's book *Family First,* I was surprised by the extent of the fears and concerns expressed in a survey of parents who responded to some items on his Web site. Seventy-five percent of these mothers and fathers expressed fear and resentment over the demands of parenthood. Many said they felt their children did not love them. They felt like they were only serving as caretakers to ungrateful, selfish dependants. Other studies have found similar results, which led me to the conclusion that great numbers of men and women in this country feel unappreciated, uncomfortable, and disappointed in their roles as parents.

Parental disillusionment escalates to alarm and fear with the first call from the principal or the police department. Parents panic when they sense they are losing control. It can be overwhelming and frightening to watch a once-loving child transform into a spiteful, self-destructive monster.

These conflicts between parents and children occur in every neighborhood in every town on every day. The irony, of course, is that love is at the center of every one of these raging parent-child battles.

We all want to be loved. We all want to give love. Yet that basic powerful human need is blocked by the walls of silence, anger, resentment, and frustration that go up between warring parents and their children.

This book is designed to bring down the walls and to restore the two-way flow of love between parents and children. My promise is to provide you with the tools to do that. But understand that the task of reaching out cannot begin until you first look within: to love and accept others, you must first love and accept yourself. This may sound scary, especially at this early stage. But I have been through this restorative process with hundreds of brave parents, and I have learned that it is never too late to learn how to love and to be loved again.

WHAT'S LOVE GOT TO DO WITH IT?

Giving and receiving love is vital to human existence. It is the glue that binds couples, families, communities, cultures, and nations. It is natural. It is instinctive. Yet this essential human capability is fragile. It can be corrupted and short-circuited to devastating effect.

Children need a loving environment to develop critical brain and organ functions. Malfunctions in the endocrine and hormonal systems and within the brain's limbic system often stem from stress due to emotional insecurities and upheaval. For example, a child who has been abused or neglected has a higher risk of acting out violently and of making bad choices because of hormonal imbalances and brain toxicity.

While we all have the natural ability to love, we are not all born with the skills and behaviors necessary to connect with others. At birth, our overriding instinct is survival, not bonding. A nursing child is looking for sustenance; the bonding is secondary. In fact, children do not have the ability to empathize with others until their fifth or even seventh year. (That is, a three-year-old cannot understand that a pinch hurts his sister just as it would hurt him.) And if something disrupts or thwarts that critical development of empathy in a child, the effects can be highly disruptive and long-lasting.

Studies have shown that individuals who lack the capacity to love and to be loved have increased risk for physical and mental problems. They even can become sociopaths, unable to function normally in society. So this is not just a family problem—it is a societal problem. And it is an adult responsibility to step up, work through the emotional challenges, and intervene; to save the child and your relationship. The benefits will last a lifetime. But to ignore the problem will only lead to far greater consequences down the road, for both of you.

A loving bond between parent and child is one of life's great gifts. But if a parent's love and care for a child are not reciprocated, for whatever reason, the lack of a connection can create utter turmoil. I've found this to be particularly challenging for the parents of children with autism and Asperger's syndrome. The divorce rate is 70 to 80 percent for those embattled families. Yet the parents of selfish, overdemanding, rebellious, and spoiled children face similar challenges.

THE PARENT TRAP

It is not hard to recognize selfish children and their devastating impact on the family. We've had many examples on the *Dr. Phil* show. I've seen many, many more in my practice. Tommy is one of the most memorable. He absolutely ran his family from the time he was six months old. He demanded his own meals, consisting of French fries, ice cream, and hot dogs, when he was two years old. His parents just wanted to avoid upsetting him, so they followed his demands to the point that his siblings were neglected. Tommy ate most of their food too.

By the time he was five years old, Tommy had used his temper tantrums to commandeer the master bedroom, sending his parents to sleep elsewhere. If any of his siblings or his parents did not follow his orders, he threatened them with a knife or gun. You can understand why this kid was a memorable challenge! But he had no major psychological problems, and his parents were of average intelligence. The mom and dad were just exhausted from dealing with this kid. It happens. Parents surrender. A study was conducted in which rat puppies wore out the mother rat by artificially imposing a continuous demand for attention without effective responses. The mother rats quickly rejected and ignored their babies, letting them die.

Rats should be expected to act like rats. But human parents also have been known to withdraw from their children when the kids become overly demanding or extremely high-maintenance. Parents aren't perfect. Often we can get trapped into repeating behaviors that only incite rebellion and resentment from our children. In one study of ADHD children, the number of positive, rewarding statements like "Good job!" made by parents to their children was compared daily to the number of negative, punishing statements they made, like "you're stupid," "you're not listening," or "you're lazy." The average number of negative statements was one hundred per day, while the average number of positive statements was calculated to be less than one per day. Granted, that study was of hyperactive kids and their exasperated parents, but every parent should be aware that what you say to your child carries more weight than you might imagine. Most children in this study said they felt abandoned and unloved by their parents. Many feared their parents.

Just as bad as "negative attention" is the wrong kind of "positive attention." Other reports show that American parents overindulge their children like no others. They shower them with toys, video games, DVDs, and other expensive distractions that may only widen the gulf and increase conflicts between parent and child. The substitution of toys for affection and love is not a new development, certainly; nor is it working any better today than it has in the past—for either party.

When parents lavish goodies upon their alienated children to "keep them busy"—a practice I describe as *boredom phobia*—they are only pouring fuel on the flames destroying their relationships. There are many ways a child can become "difficult," and it is important to be able to identify the original causes.

OVERLOADED AND OVERBOOKED

A common problem I see—and one that can really hurt the parent-child bond—is parents who hyperschedule their children's lives with nonstop activities, piling one practice upon another, one competition upon another. It's okay to get your child involved in sports, music, or other activities as long as the child derives pleasure and satisfaction from them. But too often, children are booked tighter than rooms at the Ritz. Children of all ages need downtime. They need many hours of sleep. And they need relaxed moments with their adult role models, mentors, and guides to build bonds of trust and open communication.

I suspect that parents who create frenzied schedules for their children must be doing it for themselves, because it certainly isn't for the welfare of their kids. Some adults live vicariously, pushing their children to master the things they never did. Others are hyper-competitive types who feel they have to give their children an edge. But they risk pushing their children *over* the edge instead by wearing them out, making them nervous wrecks, or robbing them of the quieter love and support they need. Too often, the message internalized by overscheduled children is that they are worthy of love only if they beat out all of their peers. What should be *unconditional* love is distorted into *transactional* love. Only by bringing home a trophy, straight A's, or the beauty queen crown can these children expect the love that should be their natural due. That is the way they come to see it. And I don't blame them.

One of the thousands of cases that reflects these downward spirals of poor bonding is that of Kay, twenty-eight-year-old mother of twelve-year-old Carla, a beautiful child who was on her way to becoming a tennis pro. Kay was determined to make her child a star. She entered Carla in every possible competition in hopes of attracting corporate sponsors, with visions of riches. She spent a fortune on trainers and equipment. She was burning through her family income and building considerable debt in her quest for love and approval. (She told me she'd spent more than $50,000 in a year just on equipment and travel expenses.) And she home-schooled her daughter so that she'd be available for training and matches.

In my sessions with this "stage mother," I could see that there was more going on. Kay seemed to feel that if she could get every-one to love her daughter, everyone would love her too.

I noted also that this little girl had learned to manipulate and control her family because of her mother's constant attention. When last I saw her, she was on her way to becoming a selfish and demanding little horror of a child. Efforts to avert that fate will have to start with the mother; the daughter will not likely change her behavior until the bond between them is no longer transactional ("your success earns my love") versus unconditional ("you'll get my love no matter what.")

TWISTED LOVE

Children hunger for love and acceptance, but their understanding of it can easily be corrupted. That is why parental love should not depend on a judgment or be awarded like a blue ribbon at the county fair. The need for parental love is so great that abused chil-dren may convince themselves that the abuse is a form of love by telling themselves, "They wouldn't care enough to hit me if they didn't love me."

Sadly, many children grow up with the notion that violence is a sign of love, and they bond on that basis. Chad's father hit him daily because he believed—and told the boy—"I am doing this for your own good so you will learn respect." Of course, this father was really teaching his son that violence was the only way to build respect. Chad grew to be a two-hundred-pound street fighter who abused his own wife and children. The great tragedy is that children who are physically and sexually abused carry their distorted perceptions of parental love into adulthood, and often become abusers themselves.

Parents also sometimes give their children food—especially sweets—as a substitute for love, which has contributed to the epidemic of obesity and diabetes among our young people. Rather than console or comfort a distraught child, some parents merely attempt to pacify them with candy or soft drinks. The problem is that "comfort food" is a poor and unhealthy alternative for true comforting, empathy, and unconditional love.

It is also true that parents who allow or encourage their children to spend hours watching television or DVDs—or wandering the Internet—are not doing their kids or themselves any favors. The development of people skills begins with interaction between parent and child—not between Nintendo and child. The kids may grow up as masters of Madden NFL Football video games, but thriving in a virtual world only isolates them and impedes the development of social skills they will need in the real world. Facebook.com is no substitute for your face at the dinner table, engaged conversation, and physical interaction. Children need to develop interpersonal skills that run deeper than typing in a screen name or instant messaging.

It cannot be said enough: *Young people learn how to relate to others through their relationships with their parents.* It all begins with you. Things may be bad between you and your children at this point. It happens. My clinic is booked months and months ahead by parents in your situation. But know this: your relationship with your children can be healed and made whole. It is going to take a great deal of effort. You will have to deal with some difficult challenges. But the rewards will last a lifetime.

My clinic, the Lawlis and Peavey PNP Center, in Lewisville, Texas, was created so that I could fulfill my dream to help children and parents create lasting, loving bonds. It is a holistic one-stop shop for repairing and building those bonds. We offer total diagnostic programs, complete medical exams, psychological analysis, cognitive studies, behavioral vision tests, and examinations for cognitive problems, family dynamics, academic learning, and neurological issues as well as individual clinical interviews. Brain scans are done to determine the level of brain function and whether toxins, allergies, and metabolic or other issues are affecting a child's behavior. With all of these critical inputs, we can design treatment programs customized to each person. Always, our goal is to make family bonds whole, and we have had remarkable success.

Pop—and Mom—Quiz

This book is designed to heal and rebuild parent-and-child relationships by working with both sides for the benefit of all parties. National divorce rates of more than 50 percent make it clear that there are many adults who lack the ability to form lasting relationships. Those who have never experienced loving parental relationships will be given the tools and direction they need to recover and become loving, caring, and involved with their children. Both sides must step up and face reality to heal the parent-child relationship. This is a warm-up exercise to give you some insights into what works and what doesn't and what is true and what is not in the tumultuous world of parents and their young.

Parents, you're up first. (Age, as they say, before beauty.) This test will offer you some insights into what is true and what is myth in regard to the parent-child relationship.

Please answer the following statements as true (T) or false (F):

1. The parental goal should be to make children happy.

   T   F

2. Television directly affects the emotional responses of a child.

   T   F

3. Cooking for your children creates emotional bonds with them.

   T   F

4. Your child will resent it if you set goals and demand they be met.

   T   F

5. Listening to music together may create bonds between you and your child.

   T   F

6. Some medications inhibit loving behavior from a child.

   T   F

7. Allowing your child to vent anger will prevent hostile behavior later.

   T   F

8. Parents often use the same child-rearing methods used by their mothers and fathers, even if they think they were ineffective.

   T   F

9. Children give love when all their needs are met.

   T   . F

10. Your child can feel loved and comforted simply by hearing your breathing patterns.

    T   F

11. A child's ability to love or be loved is determined by the physical health of the brain.

    T   F

12. Trying to reason with a child during a temper tantrum may only encourage bad behavior.

    T   F

13. To offer compliments or money for good behavior is like rewarding the child for something that should have been done anyway.

    T   F

14. Teens are in transition from childhood to adulthood and should be given freedom to experience life so they will mature more quickly.

    T   F

15. Teens act out because their brains are rewiring.

    T   F

16. Too many Christmas gifts can cause anxiety and insecurity in children.

    T   F

17. Children should be allowed to "cry it out" when they are throwing a tantrum or making a fuss.

    T   F

18. Postpartum depression can result in a failure to bond for mother and child that can cause long-term problems unless addressed.

    T   F

19. Corporal punishment is an effective way of teaching children to respect parents.

    T   F

20. A permissive parenting style encourages children to love themselves.

    T   F

Scoring

1. The parental goal should be to make children happy.

False. Children learn more quickly and feel more empathy for others when they've had to deal with disappointments and other not-so-happy circumstances. When my children tell me they are bored, I rejoice because I know they will learn to be creative. When I hear my children complain about being treated unfairly, I know there is an opportunity to develop empathy and sensitivity in them. Although it is not a scientific finding, experience suggests that children should be unhappy at least 25 percent of the time. I'm not suggesting that you set out to make their lives miserable 25 percent of the time. Life will take care of that on its own, believe me. Your job is to help them learn something positive even from negative experiences. Parents often move too quickly to solve problems for children because they do not want their darlings to suffer. That is understandable. I've been guilty of it myself. But you won't always be there to solve their problems. You need to let them develop skills and self-confidence, so they can handle challenges on their own and find ways to comfort themselves without Mommy or Daddy coming to the rescue every time.

2. Television directly affects the emotional responses of a child.

True. Every parent has witnessed this during television commercials when their kids jump up and begin reenacting the battles of their superheroes. Studies have confirmed that children mimic both the emotions and actions of characters on their television shows. If your kids constantly view young actors being aggressive and hostile toward their television parents, you can be darn sure the reality show will soon be acted out at your house. A child's ability to discriminate between life and fantasy is hazy at best. Young children are still seeking ways to interact with the world around them. Often, they perceive television as a mirror of their world, so they mimic the actions and emotions of actors just as they pick up "moves" by watching their favorite athletes perform on television.

I remember a certain seven-year-old who spent most of his time trying to kick me because he was an avid fan of the *Teenage Mutant Ninja Turtles* cartoon show, in which the shelled heroes kicked the stuffing out of the bad guys. I had to give the boy a reality check by making boundaries clear before my shins were shredded. He had to learn that striking out at authority figures is wrong, because that sort of behavior will have serious repercussions in adulthood. Still, it is possible for kids to pick up desirable behaviors from the boob tube too. Some television shows, such as *Sesame Street,* and even certain cartoons, offer polite and thoughtful characters who work together well and do honorable things. Parents should take the opportunity to offer those performers as good examples to follow.

3. Cooking for your children creates emotional bonds with them.

True. Preparing and providing meals for your child can be a bonding experience. You provide a very basic need—food—while also taking part in the ritual of eating and sharing information in a relaxed setting. Fast-food companies get this, and their ability to capitalize on the strong loyalty of young customers has fattened both their financial statements and our children. The bonds formed between children and their food sources are indeed powerful. Studies of baby monkeys have found that when frightened, they go running instinctively to their milk source—even if it is a contraption made of wire. Some quantum physicists have theorized (it is what they do, after all) that when a parent prepares a child's food, the molecules and atoms perform in different ways than when it is prepared by machines. The theory holds that these molecular differences elicit more pleasurable sensations for the child than those found even in a Quarter Pounder with cheese and super-sized fries.

4. Your child will resent it if you set goals and demand they be met.

False. The key here is to set *realistic* goals. When parents give their children attainable goals, it sends the message that you have faith in their abilities to achieve those goals—a huge confidence booster! When my high school football coach, Mr. Hinson, told me that I should be able to make the varsity football team by my sophomore year, I first thought he was crazy. But because he believed in me, I came to believe in myself. I've always been grateful that Coach Hinson believed in me at a time when it seemed no one else did.

Be warned, however, that this process can get tricky. You need to set realistic goals, but they must also be challenging enough to serve as motivation and inspiration. The parent must have a good grasp of the child's abilities and limitations. If your daughter thinks shopping is exercise, you can't demand that she run a five-minute mile. Let your child know that you want her to succeed, and chances are, she will.

5. Listening to music together may create bonds between you and your child.

True. Your musical tastes will surely differ, but if you are open to finding songs that you both enjoy, the music can bring you closer together. The rhythms of music have an impact on our brains and our emotions, and music acts as a binding force. We see it in every culture and community. It draws us together in church, in antiwar demonstrations, in military ceremonies, at weddings, and in funeral services. Your children will remember that you sang to them during those intimate hours, and remember the songs you sang together on car trips. I know of a father and a teen son who often clash, but they've found peace when listening together to Dave Matthews or Miles Davis. You may bristle at your teen's hip-hop tunes. Your teen may snarl at your country collection. But somewhere between Willie Nelson and LL Cool J there is a healing place, a common ground.

6. Some medications inhibit loving behavior from a child.

True. Medications, especially psychotropic medications, can cause drowsiness or hyperactivity. They can dull your child's emotions, and block empathy and impulse control. When a child is placed on medication, the child's mental, emotional, and social development can often be stunted. Special counseling and tutoring often is required; otherwise the child might express frustration by fighting or acting out in another way.

One of my patients, Travis, was five years old when a physician put him on a strong medication as the result of what appears to be a mistaken ADD diagnosis. During the five years he was on the medicine, Travis said he often felt "out of it." I believe the medication stunted his physical and emotional growth, and as a result he was viciously bullied. Even after being taken off the medication at the age of ten, he was emotionally immature. Once he hit puberty, he grew bigger than most of his peers, but then he became a bully because he was still locked into a child's mindset. Travis was expelled three times from junior high and high school. Later, he lost four jobs. He was very much a lost soul when I began treating him, but with coaching and counseling, he got it together. Travis is now well adjusted and serving as an officer in the U.S. Navy.

7. Allowing your child to vent anger will prevent hostile behavior later.

False. It was long taught—wrongly—that pent-up feelings of anger would fester into open rage if left restricted. Based on that wrongheaded approach, the therapeutic approach was to allow catharsis by full expression of anger. But studies have revealed that if a child is allowed to rage at his parents, the anger only builds. A child's tantrums can grow into adult violence.

A child will not find relief through expression of anger. If your child is angry, be responsible and require that any expression come with consequences. Society does not tolerate the open expression of rage without consequences. Parents need to prepare their children to live within the bounds of society.

8. Parents often use the same child-rearing methods used by their mothers and fathers, even if they think they were ineffective.

True. Unless we get training elsewhere, we tend to default to the same child-rearing patterns that our parents used. Unfortunately, we pick up and repeat both the good and the bad. Children of alcoholic parents tend to become alcoholic parents themselves. The solution is to step back, recognize your flaws or lack of parenting skills, and seek other parenting role models and approaches.

9. Children give love when all their needs are met.

False. It is your job to meet your children's basic needs, but it is also your responsibility to teach that love is not a transaction or a payoff. Your love for your child should be unconditional, and your child's love for you should be the same. The message is not: "You love me because I give you Oreos." It is: "You love me because I am your child."

How do you demonstrate this? By listening to them, but also by insisting that they listen to you. Hugs, holding hands, walking, talking, reading together, and simply being there are important. It is also necessary to be their guide, demand their respect, and, perhaps most importantly, to let them know that even when they disappoint you, your love is not withdrawn.

10. Your child can feel loved and comforted simply by the sensory stimulation of hearing your breathing patterns.

True. Nonverbal communication works in ways that science is still struggling to understand. In my counseling practice, I've often seen children calmed and comforted just by being held closely and lovingly by a parent. Studies have shown that children pick up on our moods and even mimic our breathing patterns when we hold them quietly. Bonds of trust and intimacy can be mended and established when parents are willing to drop their own fears, insecurities, and resentments and simply bring their children close to them.

11. A child's ability to love or be loved is determined by the physical health of the brain.

True. Some children have limited capacity to give or receive human affection because of their genetic makeup. Autistic children are limited in this manner, and even "normal" children can be similarly impaired by exposure to heavy metals, medications, or toxins. There is hope, however. The brain has ways of rewiring and healing itself, and there are therapies that appear to restore the ability to receive and give love. I have seen miraculous recoveries. Even those whose emotions are impeded by schizophrenia, depression, bipolarity, anxiety, and autism can be helped. Every case is different, and there are substantial challenges in each, but there is hope.

12. Trying to reason with a child during a temper tantrum may only encourage bad behavior.

True. When a child is truly upset, all reason goes out the window. Anxiety and stress short-circuit the brain by as much as 50 percent. Problem-solving abilities simply shut down. There are steps that parents can take to calm, reassure, and heal the child prone to temper tantrums. This involves first helping the child find more constructive ways to deal with frustrations and, second, communicating to the child that you understand what is going on. We all have a primary need to be understood, not managed or controlled.

13. To offer compliments or money for good behavior is like rewarding the child for something that should have been done anyway.

False. Children need positive feedback. They don't come preprogrammed to know right from wrong, good from bad. They learn from you. But they need more than punishment for doing wrong. They need to be encouraged to do right. Studies have shown that most kids are told "no" more times than they are told "yes." Without positive feedback, children feel like they've been set down in a strange land where they are supposed to learn by trial and error. Showing your child how to behave is a way to show your love. Take the responsibility for being a positive influence.

I use a "1-2-3" method of reinforcement that I learned from studying successful coaches. The steps are basic to positive motivational and transactional reinforcement and consist of:

Step one: Without anger or disapproval, explain that the child has done something wrong.
Step two: Explain two or three alternative ways of behaving that earn your approval, and could serve the same purpose or meet a goal.
Step three: Give approval and praise when the child tries to use the more positive behavior.

This more constructive approach will strengthen the bond between child and parent and help focus on the supportive basis of a relationship. It gives the child training in positive behavior instead of leaving her guessing what to do.

14. Teens are in transition from childhood to adulthood and should be given freedom to experience life so they will mature more quickly.

False. Teens can't handle too much freedom for the simple, scientific reason that their bodies and brains are undergoing significant changes that render them incapable of evaluating risk and future consequences. Their judgment is impaired. They should be held responsible for their behavior, but you can't give them too much responsibility. They need guidance and patience and love. They are not on a straight path to maturity. They've hit a detour.

15. Teens act out because their brains are rewiring.

True. As the adolescent begins the process of entering early adulthood, his brain begins a pruning process in which some connections are lost, and others are made. Up to the teenage years, their brains are in an expansion mode, and they can learn at a miraculous rate. But as they hit puberty, their brains begin to specialize. This rewiring results in reduced judgment and an inability to weigh future consequences. Those abilities are restored once the rewiring process is completed, but it can take a couple of years. Any trauma or drug abuse can extend the loss of judgment for years and even a lifetime.

16. Too many Christmas gifts can cause anxiety and insecurity in children.

True. Parents enjoy giving gifts to their children, but when gift giving becomes about quantity rather than quality, a child can become confused and anxious. Too many gifts can leave a child overwhelmed. This is especially true when a gift has special significance for a parent or family member, and they expect a certain response from the child. Most children have a hard time living up to such expectations. And it is very difficult for them to show the same appreciation for six or seven presents. It leads to frustration and anxiety. When a child appears to favor one gift and ignores others, it is simply a coping mechanism. Interestingly, as children mature, it becomes even more difficult for them to deal with multiple gifts.

17. Children should be allowed to "cry it out" when they are throwing a tantrum or making a fuss.

False. Children usually cry for a reason. When they are infants, their parents often can sense intuitively whether they are hungry, cold, fearful, or simply in need of a diaper change. When their needs are met, the crying should stop. If it does not, obviously some need has not been met.

Even the youngest children have powerful survival instincts. Infants quickly learn that crying is a means for controlling parents and getting what they want. If you always respond to crying from your child by giving him food or sweets or gifts, you are only reinforcing that controlling behavior. You need to be in control. But you also need to learn how to evaluate why your child is crying. Children should be encouraged to verbalize their reason for crying as soon as they are old enough to communicate.

18. Postpartum depression can result in a failure to bond for mother and child that can cause long-term problems unless addressed.

True. The first year is extremely important to the bonding between a child and the parent, especially the mother. However, many circumstances can disrupt this process, including postpartum depression, family conflict, and separation. But new bonds can be formed with methods I will offer.

19. Corporal punishment is an effective way of teaching children to respect parents.

False. Corporal punishment, such as spanking, is "negative reinforcement." Positive reinforcement is a much more effective tool. Negative reinforcement breaks bonds. It will not increase love, affection, and respect. Too often, parents spank their children because it gives the parents emotional release. They are striking out at the child for causing them stress and frustration. That is not a good thing. When discipline is done badly, the results are usually the reverse of what is intended. It fosters resentment, distrust, and fear. There are better ways, and I will provide you with a bunch of them.

20. A permissive parenting style encourages children to love themselves.

False. Permissive parents have the mistaken belief that if they give their children enough space and don't burden them with expectations, they will find their own way and develop self-confidence and self-love. Often, these well-intentioned but misguided parents will cite as examples Thomas Edison, Albert Einstein, or Helen Keller, who for various reasons (attention deficit disorder for Edison and Einstein, and multiple handicaps for Keller) were left to their own devices and eventually thrived. But the truth is these are the exceptions to the rule—it would be unfair to hold every child up to such high standards. There are far more examples of children floundering as adults because their parents were overly permissive. Children need guidelines. They need to know where the boundaries of behavior are. Children learn self-confidence by accomplishing goals and through loving relationships with adults. Extreme approaches to parenting tend to bring extreme behaviors in children.

Scoring Interpretation

If you scored all of these items correctly, the lessons contained in this book will be easy for you to understand and apply. But if you missed more than two, you will need to reexamine many of your perceptions of parenthood. If you missed more than five, we have some work to do, but the effort will be well worth it. I can promise all readers that the lessons and advice in this book will bring rewards that will be revealed to you over many years to come.

OVERVIEW

This book features a 90-day program designed to help you and your children learn to love and be loved by one another. It begins by offering a wealth of information and exercises that will set you on course. Each step that follows is meant to introduce skills that are essential to the healing and rebuilding of your relationships.

There are three major sections. The first tests your readiness and willingness to make a change for the better. You will learn that your child's behavior is a reflection of your parenting. Your parenting approaches will have to change to get the desired changes in your child's actions. This section also explains methods for forming loving bonds with your child and creating loving relationships at the *unconscious levels*. We look at ways to open emotional pathways that foster loving relationships. There are specials ways of touching, talking, and singing that open these pathways to create bonds quickly.

The second section is devoted to the *conscious levels* of loving behavior. We will establish critical priorities for parent-child relationships, and you will learn that the language of good parenting—the words you say to your child—echoes through a lifetime. Loving relationships have to be nurtured to grow. You will need to let go of old ideas and embrace new ones. We will explore methods for modeling self-love that hold great benefits for your child and your relationship.

The third section is inspirational. Love is not only an emotion; it is the most powerful of all human motivations. We make tremendous sacrifices because of love. We will explore the depth and the power of love and the bonds it creates between parent and child.

Most of the segments include proposed time frames for completion, based on expected motivation and effort. The exercises described in each chapter are designed to accomplish objectives for parents and children. But the time frames are suggestions, not rules. I recommend that you repeat exercises that hold special value. Take your time. Go at your own pace. Consider this an enriching experience.

Learning to love and be loved is your mission, and it is my honor to be your guide. I can teach you what you need to know. I assure you that love does conquer all. Regardless of your history, your psychological stability, your own role models, or any other challenge, I promise you that you can learn to love and to be loved. It is within your grasp, and it is the most powerful force you will ever feel.

The relationship bond is perhaps the most important treasure of life, and I have become convinced that it can be found at any time of life, but the most critical time for any important part of life is at the earliest time. A broken bond has huge consequences and costs. It can cost the child and parent the reason for life itself. Without the joy of family, much of the empowering richness of life is lacking. Loving bonds between parent and child contribute to mental, physical, and spiritual health. Such bonds are conduits for the essence of life.

2

Getting to the Roots

This is the first segment in the 90-day program, and focuses on the need for change in parental attitudes and behaviors. You will learn to love rather than "manage" your child. This segment only requires a five-day commitment, but these first steps can be critical for success.

Fifteen-year-old Hannah appeared alone one day in our office. Her mother, Mona, had dropped her off and driven away. We had to track Mona down and ask her to come back for an interview. There was no father in the picture, so the mother's input was essential, but Mona was not helpful initially. She was defensive because other therapists had blamed her for all of her child's problems. She wasn't interested in being blamed anymore, and that was understandable.

I assured Mona that we weren't in the blame business. She continued to resist our efforts to interview her. Then, when I asked her why previous agencies felt she was at fault, Mona began weeping. It was obvious that she felt tremendous guilt. Hannah had been labeled from an early age, diagnosed with ADHD and various anti-social personality disorders. She had become a heavy marijuana user, and she'd been thrown out of school repeatedly for fighting with both students and teachers. Yet even with all of those problems, Hannah was a strong student with an A average.

After interviewing her mother, I met with Hannah, who was

practically her clone. She too was short, slightly overweight, and
loaded with attitude. Still, the teen was more cooperative throughout the testing, and as we had predicted, she did well on intelligence
tests. Hannah clearly wasn't suffering from any mental problems
due to brain damage or other physical causes. But she tested high
for resentment, depression, and introversion, which meant there
was emotional turmoil under way.

During our clinical interview, Hannah opened up. It was strik-
ingly dark behind the curtain of her defiance. She considered herself
a "bad seed." Her sadness stemmed from the sense that she was a
burden to her mother. She recited a litany of sins and flaws as if they
were scars she could never remove. She had lied about some issues
in school, and she had engaged in exploratory sex with a boy,
adding to her guilt and confusion.

Hannah faltered and fell silent when I asked her if she was proud
of anything. Finally she said, "You know, I don't think I have done
anything right my whole life." Tears appeared on her cheeks, and
she quickly brushed them away as if embarrassed by any display of
vulnerability. She glumly summed up her life as a series of wrong
turns, bad moves, and hurtful incidents. She held out little hope for
her future and took no joy from her past. Hannah felt both anger
and shame toward her mother. The incidents that came to mind
included one in which she'd accidentally dropped her ice cream
cone on the ground, and her mother had forced her to pick it up and
eat it even though it was full of gritty dirt and sand. The other major
event was her discovery of her mother in bed with a man. Hannah
was too young to understand what was going on, but after that incident, Mona repeatedly accused her of having obscene thoughts. She
made her young daughter beg for forgiveness so that God would
save her from becoming a whore even though she thought like one.
It came as no surprise that Hannah felt she was destined to become
a prostitute.

Even Hannah's good grades in school gave her no hope for anything better. Her self-esteem was too low to measure. Her insights into her relationship with her mother were nonexistent. She simply shouldered all blame and assumed she was every bit as worthless as her mother.

Tragically, Mona was passing on to her daughter all of her own emotional baggage. She made no effort to deny any of Hannah's reports of emotional abuse. She had no reason to feel guilty because, for her, self-loathing was the norm. Mona had been raised within a very strict religious cult. She'd been taught that her normal thoughts were wicked and that she was doomed to eternal torture for them. She too had been subjected to severe criticism. She felt no love from either parent. Her mother left the cult and moved with Mona to a small Montana town where, to the daughter's shame, she worked as a prostitute.

Mona wept in shame and outrage as she told her story. Then she told me: "I will not allow my daughter to turn out that way. I cannot bear the shame again. You have got to stop her. I will pay you anything, but stop her, I am screwing up and I feel that I am driving her straight to hell."

This was a heart-wrenching session. It always disturbs me to see parents passing on their hurts to their children. Clearly, Mona's parenting of Hannah had been rendered toxic by her own poisoned relationship with her parents. As Mona quietly sobbed in my office, I considered how to best begin the process of helping this distraught woman love and be loved.

I asked her to repeat this emotional story to her daughter. She was resistant at first, but after we discussed it she allowed me to bring Hannah into the room. I feared a confrontation, but to my surprise, the mother and daughter sat face-to-face for a good thirty seconds without saying a word. They both wept convulsively, deeply, as if washing all of the bitterness and blame from their souls. I encouraged them to stand and hold each other for a moment. They embraced, whispering promises of forgiveness and love. I felt that we were on our way to building emotional bonds that had never had a chance to form. Sometimes, I'm overly optimistic: a week later, Hannah and Mona were at war again. Hannah came storming into my office with hurricane-force outrage, raining sheets of tears.

"I was set up! I was set up! I'm a loser! I'm such a dumb whore."

Mother and daughter shocked me when both claimed that their earlier tearful reconciliation had meant nothing.

"I still think she's going to be a whore someday," Mona said.

"So you think what you are doing is working for you?" I demanded of Mona. "Do you really think that she's going to behave differently if you don't change? Do you enjoy your self-loathing so much that it's worth ruining your daughter's life too?"

That got to her. Her eyes teared up. She stared at the floor.

"I just don't know how to change," the mother said. "I'm afraid that if I get soft with her—or with anyone—I'll get hurt. I know it's not working, but I don't know any other way. How do I stop being my own daughter's worst enemy?"

Mona's flash of insight into her own behavior gave us both something to work with. She understood the damage she was causing. I called Hannah in, and the three of us huddled in my office. It was time for a new game plan, a new approach to parenting, and a more respectful relationship between this mother and daughter.

It was clear to me from this and their earlier attempt at reconciliation that mother and daughter loved each other deeply. They had a central component necessary for mending their bond of love. But they needed a way to put it to work for them.

The plan we implemented that day did the trick—and it's that plan, essentially, that I lay out in this book. It didn't happen overnight, and it was scary for both of them because it called for breaking long-standing behaviors. We set up new rules for communicating. We established boundaries. I taught them both how to be truthful without being hurtful, and how to listen to understand rather than to respond. The healing began in earnest. Emotional and spiritual bonds were reestablished and allowed to take root and grow strong.

THE BLIND LEADING THE BLIND

It often frustrates or confuses parents when I tell them that a loving relationship is the best disciplinary tool. "Easy for you to say, Doc," is a common response.

After all, most parents feel that they love their children whether the kids are little angels or terrors in tennis shoes. But a parent can love a child without having a healthy, loving *relationship* with the child. Sometimes that love is blocked by their own family legacy, and thus, ineffective.

It works both ways, of course. Just because your children follow instructions and never act out in public doesn't mean that your relationship is a loving one. Children who fear their parents often appear well behaved, but sooner or later there is a breakdown or a backlash. Most of the parents I work with in my practice or on the *Dr. Phil* show want me to "fix" their children, as if they were cars going into Dr. Frank's Repair Shop. But most of the time it is the parent who needs a tune-up.

Your child is a reflection of your parenting, for better and for worse. If your child's behavior is not meeting your expectations, the most likely "fix" involves an adjustment in your approach. That's not a criticism. I'm not a perfect parent. Neither is Dr. Phil. I certainly don't expect anyone else to be without flaw. Even Mary and Joseph lost Jesus on a road trip, which would have gotten them a visit from a state caseworker in modern times. (Wouldn't you like to read that report? *"Parents think child walks on water. Contact Mental Health."*)

Lord knows, there are no set rules for parenting. There really aren't many rules at all. Every parent is different, and every child is different. Your parenting approach may work with one of your children but fail miserably with another. I figure that if parents get it right 67 percent of the time, they're lucky, and their kids are blessed. But the first step for every parent is to build a true loving relationship. If your child is not responding to what you are currently doing, look at other options. Many times, the answers are less complicated than you might think.

THE PARENT TRAP

I often tell my clients that their mothers and fathers know how to push their buttons because they installed them. Whether parents realize it or not, our words and actions have an enormous impact on our sons and daughters. If you don't love them, who will? If you don't trust them, who will? If you don't care enough to reach out to them, how can anyone else? This was clearly a problem in Hannah and Mona's case. The mother told her daughter she was no good, and Hannah acted accordingly.

Young people cannot learn about love and parental affection from reading a book or being told that it is so. They need to feel it, smell it, and sense it through intimate interaction. This concept can be easily corrupted by parents. The fortunate child learns of love by being cuddled, listened to, and wrapped in parental protection with words that reaffirm and reassure. The unfortunate child, tragically, learns a distorted view of love from a parent who beats or berates him, claiming "I'm doing this for your own good."

The following exercise will help you assess your own conscious and unconscious feelings about love and intimacy both as a child and as a parent. You may not be aware of some of your deeply embedded feelings—the "buttons" installed by your own parents. And even if you think you are "dealing" with those feelings by adopting a different parenting style than your parents followed, influences may be at work that you are not aware of. The goal of this assessment is to identify negative influences and deal with them so that you can be the loving parent you aspire to be. Respond to the questions honestly. This is a crucial first step in the healing process.

YOUR LOVE LEGACY ASSESSMENT

This exercise will require you to assess where and when in your childhood you formed your own definitions of love and affection. To be a loving parent, you need to fully understand where your parenting approach originated. Be honest about your experiences and what you perceived. As you work through this exercise, you will see that some questions seek longer responses than others. The more details you provide, the more helpful this exercise will be.

1. How did your mother show you that she cared about you?
2. How did your father show you that he cared about you?
3. What were the primary values emphasized by your parents? (Examples: hard work, honesty, loyalty, always being right, getting even, and so on.)
4. When you did not get your way initially as a child, what did you do next? Did it work?
5. What values were stressed as your "family values"?
6. What were your mother's worst qualities as a parent?
7. What were your father's worst qualities as a parent?
8. What was the worst part of your relationships within the family?
9. What were your parents' worst fears for your future?
10. How did your parents react to your achievements and happiness?

11. How did you learn to work with others to achieve a common goal?

12. Whose parenting style (mother, father, others) have you adopted? Why?

ASSESSING YOUR LEGACY: FOUR GUIDING QUESTIONS FOR POSITIVE PARENTING

This exercise is not about making judgments about your parents, or condemning their parenting style or yours. It simply gives you the opportunity to reflect on the influences and role models that are reflected in your own parenting. Look at your answers and consider the influences and role models that you noted. Are some of them negative? Have some caused problems? Which are worth keeping, and which should be discarded? Are you doing things with your child in response to what your parents did to you? Are they working or not working?

The following four questions will help you home in even more on the underlying factors that influence your parenting style. These are questions you will be continually asking yourself, so make a habit of it. Are your parenting methods based on:

1. Truths or myths?
2. Positive or negative reinforcement?
3. Natural consequences?
4. Long-term relationship building?

Truths or Myths

Your parenting methods are rooted in your memories of how your parents treated you. Since our perceptions and conclusions about the world are based on those memories, we can get trapped into a system of thinking that is based solely on myth. As children, we remember things differently, even those events we consider to be critical to the development of our personalities. Ask yourself if your memory is accurate, and whether it serves you well; or does it serve up myths that are detrimental to your relationships? For example, one parent I counseled vividly remembered his father coming home drunk every night, but his older sister said that their father had come home intoxicated only once, and it had led to a traumatic incident. Whatever happened, the brother and sister were deeply impacted, and each carried the memory with them into adulthood.

It is a psychological fact that our memories are riddled with distorted perceptions. They tend to be based 90 percent on our feelings and needs. Eyewitnesses in court proceedings are notorious for not remembering details in the same way. It is easy enough to counter the evidence of an eyewitness by presenting another one. In most cases, including my own, memories tend more toward myth than reality. That is why counseling is helpful. A professional therapist can help you separate myth from reality. If we base our parental philosophies on childhood memories, we risk sailing into parenthood with distorted maps that may lead us astray. The man who carried memories of his father as a drunk adopted a very controlled manner of behavior and an extremely strict command-and-control style of parenting, based on what proved to be a false impression from his own childhood. Through counseling, he learned to accept the truth that his father had suffered from severe depression. As a result, he lightened up on himself and his children, creating stronger, more loving bonds.

Kids don't come with an operating manual—not even Cliffs-Notes or a For Dummies guide. So it is not surprising that many parents go about raising their children based on myths that have been handed down by their parents and grandparents. Here are some of the most common myths of parenthood that can interfere with the creation of lasting, loving bonds:

- My children naturally love me because I'm their parent.
- My father/mother was very tough on me, and I am what I am today because of it. I will do the same for my children, and they will love me for it later.
- I am going to give my children everything I didn't have, and they will love me for it.
- I am going to tell my children I love them every day so they will know what unconditional love is.
- My children know that I love them because I pay for everything, and I put them to bed every night.
- Guilt is a good way of teaching children how to be grateful and appreciative.
- My children owe me, so they will make good grades and perform well in sports and activities.

All of these myths are based on false or shallow assumptions. They come from the thousands of stories heard by theorists like myself, and they have nothing to do with how children's minds actually work. They have served to do tremendous damage to love bonds.

How do we know the truth? This is the process of self-assessment and awareness. You have to challenge your beliefs and the sources for them every day of your life. This is often the goal in psychotherapy, especially psychoanalysis. It is time to revisit the myths and truths you have based your life and family values on.

The Bible teaches that you should take the "log out of your eye" before criticizing another's perception of the world, and that the truth shall set you free. The Buddha explained that we see the world only through the mirrors of our eyes, and the enlightened one is the one with the least distortion in those mirrors. Every religion I know has some mention of this process, so it must be important in many arenas.

Positive or Negative Reinforcement

Children have to be taught socially acceptable behaviors. This is not instinctual. Behavior reinforcement is one of the basic tools of psychology. At its most basic level, it involves changing behaviors by giving or withholding rewards. Desirable behaviors occur more frequently if they are rewarded, which is known as positive reinforcement. Negative reinforcement is used to stop or decrease undesirable behaviors.

Most children learn best through a combination of positive and negative reinforcements. If Johnny is running around the house, you could give him a punishment: "No television until you settle down." Or you could offer a reward: "If you settle down, I'll let you watch television tonight." When he behaves as desired, you reward him with more reinforcement.

It's a fairly simple concept, yet I've often observed parents reinforcing undesirable behavior because they don't understand how reinforcement works. Many parents complain to me that the time-out tactic doesn't work for their children. Often, it is because they send the little rascals off to serve their time-outs in a playroom or bedroom packed with a television, stereo, toys, and other amusements. Now that's hard time! It's like punishing a kid by sending him to Disneyland.

I've got another pet peeve in the parental reinforcement department. Many times, I've witnessed children rudely interrupting their parents during a conversation with another adult. All too often, the parents deal with it by halting the conversation and then spending several minutes telling the child how bad it is to interrupt. But what has actually happened in this case? What has been reinforced? The wrong behavior! The child has succeeded in interrupting, and the parent has reinforced the rudeness by focusing all attention on the offending child.

Instead of rewarding the disruptive behavior with attention, offer a more constructive avenue for what both of you want. The message to get across is: Do not interrupt me while I am talking. If the child wants some attention, you can hold her hand or rub her shoulders while you finish your discussion. As the child gains the ability to wait for an appropriate time for attention, you can reward her with praise and support. Delay of reward and patience can be a major accomplishment for anyone.

Behavior reinforcement is not difficult to master. But studies have shown that parents who claim to have problems with their children rarely use positive reinforcement. Often these parents report that their children already know what is expected of them, but they are acting out. I've found that parents often put pressure on their children to "act right" when they haven't taken the time to give proper guidelines for behaving.

My clinic conducted a study in which we asked a group of parents to take one day and record every instance in which they addressed their children either negatively or positively. The results were rather amazing, especially in the cases of children with troubled behavioral histories. Most of these statements were pretty mild, such as "Stop that" or "You are making Mommy mad." But there were many statements that made my flesh crawl:

- "You're stupid."
- "You better stop that, or I'll tear your arms off."
- "I think you're psycho, and I'm calling the cops right now to take you to jail."
- "I am telling Santa Claus, and you won't get nothing."

Sadly, the number of positive statements were few. Esteem-boosting statements such as "You are such a good girl when you do that" and "Good job" were few and far between.

Now imagine how you would feel if all you got from your boss came out of the Blame, Shame, and Frame file. Children don't learn love for themselves from that sort of feedback. You can expect their only responses to be anger, frustration, fear, and rebellion.

Unfortunately, we have rarely been taught how to give positive reinforcement. The first concept we have to learn is the "currency" value of what we can offer as reinforcement, and whether we actually have the power and resources to use it as a reinforcer. For example, children under the age of seven usually go for physical treats like candy and events like swimming and zoo visits. They also value social reinforcers like praise and acknowledgment of accomplishments. If Jimmy behaved well in school, it is good to acknowledge how well he did. You can do this by giving him a treat for his good behavior, and/or telling him how proud you are of him. Children are natural people-pleasers, so this usually goes over big.

As the child gets older, it is harder to find currency. Candy isn't high on the list with teenagers. They are more interested in social rewards such as the opportunity to interact with friends, or to participate in sports, music, or other favorite activities. As simple as this concept of positive reinforcement may be, parents often resist it. It is common to contend that kids shouldn't be rewarded for doing what they should be doing. But that stance assumes, falsely, that kids always know what the "correct" behavior is.

Parents object, "Nobody gives me anything for behaving at my job. Nobody rewards me with cookies when I do the laundry or cook a good meal." Yet we all behave on a reinforcement system. We get paid a salary or wage for behaving on our jobs. We get affection and praise for helping others. We get compliments when we dress well. I would agree, however, that adults often don't get enough reinforcement, except on Mother's Day and Father's Day.

Most of the time, we all act in our own interests. When we do something unselfish, it is generally because of our internal systems of reinforcement. We set "standards" for ourselves as guidelines. Where do these standards come from? Mostly from our early training and reinforcement provided by parents.

Natural Consequences

In most of the cases we see at my counseling center, parents have no concept of "natural consequences" even though they have to live with them. Typically, they punish bad behavior as a reaction to their own anger and frustration. That doesn't work, especially when you want a loving bond with your child. For every action there is an equal and opposite reaction in forces. Natural consequences are those that follow an event. They can be interpersonal as well as physical. If you pinch your boss on the butt—a severe breach of office etiquette—you can naturally expect a severe consequence that will involve your being fired or disciplined (unless, of course, you and the boss have a special relationship).

Too often, parents deliver consequences that don't fit their children's actions. Rather than simply reacting to bad behavior and doing the first thing that comes to mind, parents should make certain that the child understands what he has done wrong—and then levy a consequence that is appropriate. It takes time and thought to do that, and too many adults aren't willing to make the effort.

During my tenure as a junior high school teacher, I set up a special class for kids who were particularly disruptive. Mostly, they were just mouthing off. Giving them detentions was the standard punishment, but it had no effect on their behavior. So I made them go to a class on conflict resolution instead. It was a huge success. Not only did the kids learn more efficient methods for resolving their issues with teachers, they also felt that they had served their "sentence" for their offenses in a constructive manner. They got it.

Long-term Relationship Building

To build a sensitive and mutually caring relationship with your child, you must make it clear that your goal is to cooperate rather than to dictate. Often, the battles between parents and children are over control and who is "right." But you can be right all the time and destroy your relationship in the process, so what good does that righteousness do you? A parent's job is not to be right and win every battle. That command-and-control approach may be necessary for military leaders, but your mission is to mold a caring and responsible human being, not a fighting machine.

Jenny, sixteen, and her mother, Rhonda, came to me because they were locked in battle over Rhonda's rules for dating and curfews. Jenny wanted her curfew hours extended on weekends so she could stay out later with friends and boyfriends. She pointed out that most parties didn't even begin until 10:00 p.m. or later. Rhonda would not budge, reasoning that there were more potential threats to her daughter's safety during the late hours on weekends than during the week. Both the mother and daughter felt they had strong arguments. Rhonda had the advantage, of course, since she had the power, not to mention the car keys. But the tension with her daughter wore on them both.

Rhonda's history explains the underlying tension in her relationship with her daughter. She ran away from home at the age of fifteen because she was always in conflict with her parents. She is the middle child, sandwiched between an industrious brother who is a computer wiz and a super-student sister who is a superior athlete. Rhonda considered herself the family's black sheep. Her lack of self-esteem and poor bonds with her own family have left Rhonda with few parenting tools. Her own fears and anxiety were interfering with her ability to be a loving mother to her daughter.

My question was simple: "Rhonda, is this approach working for you? Are you getting what you want?"

She was in battle mode. She squared off at me as if I was siding with the enemy: "I'm not getting what I want, but at least she isn't getting what she wants."

That summed up her command-and-control approach succinctly.

I let her words sink in for a few seconds, and then I asked her, "Is this approach accomplishing your goal? Or are you merely trying to keep her from accomplishing hers? For now, you have the power. But when she hits eighteen, she'll be out the door—and the only thing she'll have learned about resolving conflicts in relationships is to flee them. Is that what you want for her?"

Rhonda looked away, still angry, still frustrated, still fighting the urge to command and control. I could sense her inner torment. I let her stew for a good fifteen minutes. She was going through her sparsely equipped maternal toolbox. Finally, she admitted that she needed help.

"What can I do and still be a mom?"

And with that, we began the process of equipping Rhonda with tools for building a bond with her daughter. The secret ingredient was *listening*, hearing Jenny's needs and emotions rather than focusing on her words. By listening to understand—rather than to respond—Rhonda came to realize that her daughter was a person who wanted love and guidance. Rhonda discovered mothering instincts she never knew she had. She learned to express her protective feelings. She told Jenny why she was worried about her being out late instead of simply forbidding her to be out past curfew. She didn't just lay down the law; she explained herself and in the process created mutual understanding.

I also encouraged Jenny to express her own need for love. She told Rhonda how much she appreciated having her as a mother, and that she still would strive to show respect and caring for their relationship. But she wanted respect in return.

With this understanding Rhonda and Jenny found common ground. They negotiated an agreement in which Jenny promised to demonstrate responsible behavior by using a cell phone to keep in touch. She became more mindful of her mother's concern for her. Rhonda demonstrated her love with a more respectful form of supervision. Mutual understanding and cooperation replaced suspicion, mistrust, and constant tension.

I helped Rhonda see that she could give up ground and the "right to be right" and still win long-term victories that would strengthen the loving bonds. There would still be conflicts, of course. But by setting reasonable boundaries and making consequences clear, Rhonda helped Jenny develop lifelong relationship skills. They formed a bond reinforced with self-awareness and openness. Years later, Jenny and her mother looked back on the conflicts of her teen years and laughed at themselves and their head-butting. But if they had not found the tools for resolving conflicts, their bitterness and anger could easily have endured for decades, even for their lifetimes, and into the next generation as well.

OVERINDULGED AND DANGEROUS

The command-and-control parenting approach can backfire, but other parents swing too far the other way, making the mistake of putting all the power in the hands of their ill-prepared children. After a series of violent incidents at home and school, thirteen-year-old Mark walked into my office under a court order for a psychological examination. The judge was inclined to send him to reform school, and he had a strong case. Mark's baggage included drug abuse, trouble in school, sexual promiscuity, and rebellion against authority. His mother, single parent Janna, had backed all of his excuses. She tried to explain his self-destructive behavior by noting that he'd been overweight and self-conscious, picked on by other kids, and misunderstood by his teachers.

As Janna built the pedestal for him to stand on, Mark smirked and basked in her cluelessness. I finally sent him out of the room to control the damage. Still, Janna went on reciting her well-rehearsed justifications for her son's shortcomings. She had one thing right: Mark was a victim. He'd been set up to fail. But it was by his mother—not his teachers, his schoolmates, or an uncaring cast of authority figures.

Of course, Janna came out of her own troubled history. Her parents were drug addicts and barely qualified as guardians. Her Christmas meals were provided by the Salvation Army. Any gifts she got came from charitable organizations because her parents spent their money on their habits. Somehow Janna had emerged from this environment with her capacity to love still intact. But she had no frame of reference for parenting properly. She'd been deprived of her parents' love, so she lavished hers upon her only son. Her parents had withheld childhood toys, Christmas presents, and birthday gifts, so she spent every penny she had to make certain Mark got everything he wanted—and more. Stacked in his bedroom were unopened presents from Christmases past.

Given the incredible levels of his mother's overindulgence, it was remarkable that Mark functioned as well as he did. The kid might easily have become a raging little despot, but as it was, he was a good-looking boy who could turn on the charm and charisma when it served his purposes. Those skills made him all the more dangerous in some ways because when he self-destructed, he was likely to do a lot of emotional pain to those who had trusted him. Janna had indulged her son to the point that he had a two-year-old's view of the universe. He saw himself as the center of all things. The rest of the human race was there to serve his needs, just as his mother had.

After extensive interviews with this mother and son, I told the judge that I didn't think Mark would derive much benefit from reform school. Instead, I recommended enrollment for six months to a year in an excellent drug rehabilitation program in Kerrville, Texas. I also recommended that, as a condition of her son's probation, Janna be required to enroll in a parental training program. I told her that Mark's behavior would change only if she was willing to change the way she parented him.

At the end of six months, Mark seemed little inclined to give up his self-centered view of the world. But thankfully, his mother had seen the light and undergone an amazing transition. I had worked with her to improve her parenting skills. She realized that she'd been "addicted to child spoilin'." She even called herself a "recovering Mom addict." (A sense of humor can be an extremely useful tool for parents.) Janna's awakening was assisted by a support group of other mothers with similar problems. She had backup. And spoiled little "Marky boy" never knew what hit him.

When he returned home from the drug rehab program, Mark discovered a "Cooperation List" on the refrigerator. It offered a very clear explanation of the rewards and the consequences of both good and bad behaviors. He learned that freedoms and privileges that he had long taken for granted would now be awarded only if he cooperated with his mother and followed her rules. Mark also found that his mother had new parenting muscle. The boy rebelled at first, which was fully expected. But Janna and her backup team were prepared for it. She had learned to take the long view. Rather than indulging her son's need for immediate and continuous gratification, she held out for the lifelong benefits of a son who understood that the world did not revolve around him.

This was a tough case. Mark had been wired from infancy with a self-centered view of the world, and it is usually very difficult to fix that. But, to my surprise, he responded well. He learned to be cooperative and less self-centered. I saw him grow into a rather remarkable adult who used his charm and good looks to reach out and help others instead of for his own selfish reasons. While he'd once seemed totally self-absorbed and bound for self-destruction, Mark redirected his considerable energies toward earning top grades, getting a law degree, and—amazingly—becoming a dedicated public servant. I never would have predicted it, but Mark served as mayor of his small community, and by all accounts, he was a good one.

PREPARE FOR THE CHALLENGE—AND THE REWARDS

Sometimes the power of good parenting exceeds even my expectations. But it often takes parents who are committed to taking difficult and even emotionally painful steps. Now is the time to ask yourself: Are you willing to take the steps necessary to build loving bonds with your child?

The following questionnaire is intended to assess your willingness to change in order to get the results you desire. Building a loving relationship requires focus, time, effort, and high levels of self-awareness. You must make rebuilding your relationship with your child a priority project.

Consider the following statements and your willingness to follow through with them.

I am willing to:

1. Honestly assess my parenting methods and their effectiveness in building long-term loving bonds with my child.
2. Begin planning for and building a long-term relationship based on cooperation and mutual respect.
3. Clarify the family values we will use to set standards of behavior.
4. Assess the issues from my own past that might be adversely affecting my parenting style, and make constructive changes.
5. Consider that my parenting style might be based on myths that I need to discard.
6. Use positive reinforcement as a foundation for my parenting style.
7. Listen to my child with the goal of understanding rather than reacting.
8. Spend more time talking and interacting with my child, and not letting emotions rule our time together.

9. Accept that my child's interests may not match my expectations.
10. Make it my daily mission to find something positive and enlightening about my child.

THE PLAN

The time for blaming, regretting, and apologizing is over. You are officially in the rebuilding stage. You can learn from the past, but you can't change it. Today is a new day, and we cannot waste energy on what might have been. What's done is done. Put it behind you and cast your eyes forward to the future. If you are willing to change approaches that have not worked, and if you are committed to building long-term, loving relationships with your children, then here are your next steps:

Day 1: Step Up and Be the Role Model Your Child Needs

Now and then a parent tells me, "I don't want to be a hero to my child. I want them to see me as I am so they can be better than I am." This is a cop-out. You can't shuck the responsibility of serving as an example and role model. It comes with the kid's birth certificate. To build a lasting, loving bond with your child, you have to live up to your end of the parental contract. You've got to stand up and give it your best at all times.

Most parents don't realize that they are the most important figures in their children's lives from day one. Your children know more about you than you know about yourself. Your child has been studying and responding to you from the age of one month. Babies instinctively pick up on parental moods. As children grow older, they learn to judge what their parents' responses will be based on moods, facial expressions, tone of voice, and other subtle clues.

Through the years, your child's instinctive manipulations grow more sophisticated. A child will learn that one parent may be easier to manipulate when sad, while another parent is likely to lash out in a similar mood. Children also take responsibility for their parents' moods, even for the breakup of a marriage or a family's financial problems. So it is critical that you understand just how important you are in your child's life. You are their guide to the world. Early in life, they depend on you for their most basic needs. But they never stop needing your approval and guidance. You need to be at your best so that your child mirrors the best that you have to offer.

Your child will sense that you don't care enough to try. You do not have to be perfect. You only have to give it your best effort. Express your love by trying your best for your child and the child will do the same for you.

Define what kind of hero you will be. What values are you going to stand for? List them and describe what kind of behavior and circumstances would demonstrate this value for your child:

- Value: _____
  Behavior and theoretical or real circumstances that would demonstrate this value to your child: _____
  _____

- Value: _____
  Behavior and theoretical or real circumstances that would demonstrate this value to your child: _____
  _____

- Value: _____
  Behavior and theoretical or real circumstances that would demonstrate this value to your child: _____
  _____

Day 2: Walk Your Talk

The old adage holds true: If you don't stand for something, you will fall for anything. The effort and courage you put into following these values communicates their importance to your children. I am always alarmed when a child tells me, "My family isn't any different from anyone else's." Your children need to know that there are values and principles and other guidelines that they are expected to follow.

Children get into trouble when they don't have guidelines. It is your job to provide those guidelines. They don't know right from wrong any more than they know left from right—unless you tell them. You have to give them a foundation for making informed decisions. They will be tempted, coerced, and led astray by others. It is your job to build in a self-correcting system.

What are the truths and standards by which you try to run your life? If you have not clearly set standards for conduct, they have no way of measuring. Until they are mature adults, they need guidance, and they will follow your example, whether it is good or bad. Do you ever lie to get your way? Do you have a clear concept of justice? Do you ever settle personal conflicts by making threats or by seeking a common ground? Is it ever right to break the rules at school? Is it smart and cute to mouth off to authority?

A caution: If you fail to live up to your established standards, then you'd better be willing to explain yourself. Children can spot hypocrisy with amazing speed. If you don't walk the talk, they will call you on it, and they will want to know why they should follow guidelines that you ignore.

Today, hold a formal family meeting to make your standards clear. Ask for their suggestions. You'll be surprised at their need for limits and guidelines. I recommend no more than five main rules. I have just three suggestions for my own children:

- Love is the reason we do all we do.
- Justice and fairness must prevail.
- Truth is the only response.

Days 3–4: Open the Lines of Communication

Believe it or not, children secretly want to put down the video game controllers and talk to you. They want to share their lives with you, and they want to know what is on your mind, but they are waiting for signs that you are listening. The other day my daughter began regaling me about her puppet show featuring Dr. Do-Good and Stuffy. Do I care about Dr. Do-Good or Stuffy? Sure, I care, but only because of what they mean to my daughter. I listened to her intently, not to what she was saying so much as to what she was telling me through her emotions, gestures, and level of excitement. I consciously listened to understand, not to respond. And that is a very important thing for every parent to do.

Right now, at this early stage of her life, my daughter doesn't have a lot of information that I haven't heard, but she does have things to say that are important. It is critical that we continue to communicate and listen to each other because within five or six years, those lines of communication are going to be very important. One day my daughter will want to talk to me about something that will have major significance in our lives. When that day comes, I want there to be a foundation of mutual trust and understanding so she feels free to speak to me and so I will listen and understand.

Communication skills don't just come to you and your child when needed. We all have to practice talking, kids and parents alike. Parents have to learn how their children express themselves and how to measure the importance of what they are saying. And we must demonstrate that we care enough to listen with understanding and compassion.

I can't tell you how many times I've sat with distraught parents and their needy children in a drug intervention center, or a juvenile detention center, and watched them struggle to communicate with each other as if for the first time. It's not just sad, it's telling. Parents who have long-established and open lines of communication with their children are far less likely to end up in such tragic situations.

Let's go to the communication lines. Open them up. Take all calls, however meaningless, silly, juvenile, or preposterous. One day, your child will want to tell you something that could make the difference between success and failure, even life and death. Think long-term. Put the newspaper down. Hang up the telephone. Listen and understand.

Take thirty minutes one day to just listen and talk to your child. Ask questions, ask about how she feels, and just have fun in her world. See if you can find out what two good things happened to her during the day, and what things happened that might not have been so good.

The next day have another discussion with your child and see if there are any consistencies about how she feels, or the good or bad things that happened. She will need to practice talking with you, so be prepared to share your day with her as well.

Day 5: Always Find a Common Ground

Just as it is critical to communicate with your child, it is also vital that you establish a negotiating forum that allows both sides to walk away winners. Conversations should never be about losing. They should be about reaching an understanding that benefits you both. It's best to establish the negotiating method early on. You can make a game of it, but always working toward the win-win. I've used one of the most popular children's games, rock-paper-scissors, as a way to establish a cooperative spirit. In my version, everyone wins. Instead of the rock-paper-scissors symbols, each person extends one to five fingers, representing numbers. If the total number of fingers displayed between both players equals six, each is a winner and celebrates. If the number is different, no one wins and another trial is repeated. Another win-win game involves tossing a ball into the air. If one of you catches it, everyone wins. But if no one catches it, you keep trying.

Today I want you to play a game with your children, one in which everyone can rejoice. It may be a card game or one of the many board games, but when a person gains a point or two, everyone rejoices. Even if it is a competitive game and you might have sacrificed a point, rejoice with the winner. It is not who wins or loses, it is the shared enthusiasm in support of each other.

These are simple exercises, but the lesson is important: the best victory is a shared one. You can emphasize this cooperative spirit in group activities like washing the car, building a clubhouse, preparing a meal, or digging for a garden in the backyard. It's good to create family activities so that when the family needs to come together for a crisis, there is already a foundation of mutual cooperation and support. I advise parents of young children to devise at least one activity per month in which you practice collaboration and cooperation.

DECISION TIME

At this point, you should have a good feel for what lies ahead in this book. I have not sugarcoated the challenges or the amount of work that will be needed. Do you care enough to continue? I believe you do, and I promise that you will find the tools you need. But only you can make the commitment required to create loving bonds that will last a lifetime for you and your children. Let's turn the page, literally and figuratively, and begin a new path, so that you never again have to lie in bed overcome with regrets and fears because you weren't the parent your child needed you to be.

3

Nature versus Nurture

The second segment in the 90-day program looks at the most powerful of human survival instincts and how we all tend to revert to these instincts when threatened in some way. You should give yourself ten days, including two weekends, to complete this section. It will help you to understand natural and instinctual behavior in your children as survival mechanisms rather than as "acting out" behavior to be feared or condemned.

One of the messages I repeat to parents every day is that they have two primary responsibilities toward their children:

1. To applaud their talents and dreams.
2. To give them the social skills essential to surviving and thriving as contributing members of society.

Children need both our encouragement and our guidance. They are not fully formed when born. In fact, some of the instincts they are born with can hinder social development and parental bonding. It has been popular in some circles to suggest that given a free, supportive environment—one unimpeded by adult interference—children will grow into perfectly formed beings. Such stories are found throughout human history: from ancient Rome and the tale of the twins Romulus and Remus, who were raised by wolves, to Sumerian mythology, in which Enkidu lived with gazelles. They have given rise to modern legends, including Pecos Bill, the cowboy raised by wolves, and of course Tarzan, the king of the jungle raised by apes.

Unfortunately, research has shown that children raised without adult supervision don't fare all that well in the real world. There have been actual cases of "feral children" who were lost or abandoned and survived on their own. But those who get no adult care before the age of five never learn to speak human language, and their hygiene habits never mature to socialized levels. Those found at younger ages are capable of some socialization, but they do not ever function as independent adults. Their priorities remain extremely basic: food, shelter, and self-interest only.

Human survival instincts are powerful. They rule our behaviors until we are socialized and learn to function in the world. Children who do not receive the right degree of this socialization will suffer, and cause others to suffer as well.

SURVIVOR INSTINCTS

Pete was eight years old when his parents brought him to my clinic for an assessment. My first impression was that the parents must have brought the wrong child. He smiled, laughed, and appeared at first observation to be a very clever, good-natured boy. His grades were high. He'd had no behavioral problems in school, and he was cooperative with my staff. But his parents expressed concern about Pete's hostility and aggressiveness toward his six-year-old brother. They were frightened that Pete would hurt him. They expressed fears of leaving Pete alone because of the "demon inside him."

That demon was nowhere to be found in our initial interviews with the boy, but once we learned more, I began to understand. Pete functioned normally around everyone except his brother. We dug deeper into his records and found that Pete had been adopted at the age of one from an orphanage. Agency records—which cannot always be trusted—claimed that he'd been a well-behaved child up to that point. Apparently he adjusted well to his adoptive mother and father and had no problems until the second child, Perry, was adopted two years later.

Pete was hostile toward Perry from the start. He pestered and hit him until he cried. His parents attempted to deal with it by giving him time-outs in his playroom-bedroom, and by rewarding good behavior with more toys and treats. The parents also did their best to give Pete individual attention, and that seemed to alleviate some of his aggressiveness toward Perry at first. But then Pete took to sneaking into Perry's room at night and attacking him. He seemed determined to eliminate Perry from the family picture.

Pete's behavior was intolerable, of course, but also quite under-standable in terms of human survival instincts. As a child reared in an orphanage, Pete had to compete for essentials like food, comfort, and adult attention. His survival instincts were sharply honed in that environment. As a cute and clever kid, he learned to use both his charm and his cunning. His adoption made life much easier as long as he was the only child. Naturally, he was not thrilled when Perry showed up. His new brother came from the same orphanage, and it's possible that Pete's hostility was increased by familiar scents from that environment.

So Pete was not possessed by any demons other than very strong survival instincts developed in what he perceived to be a somewhat hostile childhood environment. He wasn't evil. He was doing what he felt was necessary for his own survival, but this behavior had to be curtailed for the long-term survival of all parties.

The big challenge for Pete's parents was to teach him that he had more to gain by accepting his brother than by throttling him. Like all children (and some adults), Pete needed to realize that his brother could be a valuable ally rather than an enemy. Our challenge was to teach Pete to trust and accept other children by showing him that loving relationships provide more security than aggressive, hostile relationships. Pete had entered the world in an environment that encouraged him to develop a "scarcity mentality." He thought that he had to grab all the food, water, toys, and adult affection he could because there was only so much of it to go around. We had to teach him an "abundance mentality" by showing him that there was plenty for everyone.

I instructed his adoptive parents to create games in which Pete and his brother would be rewarded for working together rather than individually. We set up bicycle races between groups of six- and eight-year-olds in which they competed as teams for cumulative scores. Both boys enjoyed golf, so we also had them play as a two-man team against other kids. Pete was very smart and highly competitive, so his instincts at first were to prove his superiority even as a team player. It took him several months to embrace his brother as a teammate rather than view him as a competitor or a threat.

Fortunately, other natural instincts kicked in as the brothers bonded. It was a joy to see them discovering ways to work together, playing to each other's strengths and supporting each other. Pete was not as speedy on a bike, but Perry helped him by running interference for him and keeping other bikers behind them. Pete was the better golfer, but he coached and encouraged Perry to improve his game. Without intervention and guidance, Pete might well have taken a nine iron to the head of his younger brother one day, so his acceptance of and support for Perry was truly a wonderful development.

Nearly a year after we first met Pete, the brothers visited the clinic to show off their trophies and ribbons. I took Pete aside and asked him how things were going. His answer was moving: "I always wanted to be adopted so I could have a family. But I understand now that you have to learn to be a family. It doesn't just happen. My parents, even my brother and I, are family now."

NATURE VERSUS NURTURE

Whenever a child shows lack of respect for authority and a resistance to working and playing with others, it should trigger alarms. Too often selfish behavior is ignored or even indulged. Children need guidance if they are to learn to work and thrive in society, and if they are to know the joy of loving, long-term relationships.

Zoologist and anthropologist Lyall Watson says in his book *Dark Nature: A Natural History of Evil* that the basis of evil lies at the heart of our survival as a species. Even evil acts—murder, lying, stealing—have been justified in some cases as necessary for survival. Humans are not alone in their keen survival instincts, of course. The animal world provides us with the most ferocious examples of powerful survival instincts. One of the most striking examples is that of siblings in the hyena family. To be accused of laughing like a hyena is an insult, but believe me, these beasts have worse traits.

Hyenas are always born in pairs as identical twins, with full sets of razor-sharp teeth and razor-sharp survival instincts. Within an hour of birth, the twins are engaged in combat to establish dominance. Because their mother stashes them in aardvark burrows while she feeds them from the mouth of the burrow, the cub that loses the battle usually dies of starvation, if not from its wounds, because it can't get past the dominant cub to its food source. Such fierce sibling rivalry is not unusual in the wild. Baby herons fight over every minnow dropped into the nest. Black eagle chicks have been known to peck each other to death. And a flock of baby chicks is no place for, well, chickens.

The drive to survive is likely embedded in the genes of most creatures, including humans, of course. Often it seems the deadliest wars are those fought to preserve the genetic or philosophical strains of heritage. Global warfare, civil wars, turf battles, and family feuds are often about the advocates of one civilization, one culture, one religion, or one way of life trying to dominate or eradicate another. Fratricide and siblicide are more common than we might care to acknowledge, forming the tragic basis for historical accounts, legends, myth, and folklore from Cain and Abel to *East of Eden*.

Alfred Adler, one of the founders of psychoanalytic thinking, who later developed his own school of therapy, practiced primarily with children. He noted this "need for superiority" among the young and coined the term *inferiority complex* to imply the internal source of motivation to survive and gain power in a social context. His contributions to child psychology in his study of survival struggles among children have been profound. Interestingly, Adler defined the ultimate survival skill that children should be taught as cooperation. He also identified four destructive behavioral patterns that children exhibit toward parents: seeking revenge, struggling for power, vying for attention, and feigning incompetence.

- **Revenge** involves striking back at perceived abuse or injustice.
- **Power-struggling** involves a child attempting to usurp parental authority and establish control.
- **Attention-getting** is marked by distractive behavior rooted in deeper issues. Bed-wetting is often an attention-getting behavior that signals more serious issues.
- **Incompetence-feigning** involves a child pretending to be incapable of something in order to avoid doing it: "I can't tie my shoes" or "I can't be nice to my sister."

All of these are self-centered behaviors triggered, to some degree, by survival instincts that put the individual's drives and needs above all else. And all are parental nightmares. The "me first" attitude becomes perhaps most exasperating in the teenage years, when children may look like adults and often demand adult freedoms but remain incredibly self-centered, in the manner of small children who think the world revolves around them. Fortunately, most teens grow out of that aggravating attitude, but some do not. Some grow into adulthood focused on their own wants and needs, lacking the social skills necessary to build relationships or the networks that are vital to career success. Tragically, these people often spend the last years of their lives in isolation too. Research has found that male "loners" have abbreviated life expectancies. Our challenge is to break the pattern of instinctive selfishness and to give our children the tools to love and be loved, to trust and be trustworthy, to care and be caring.

Nurturing a Cooperative Spirit

Loving relationships are built on selflessness and cooperation. The selfish, antisocial child will have great difficulty experiencing mature loving relationships. Sadly, I see many parents failing to encourage and develop cooperation and selflessness in their children. The following questionnaire will help you assess whether or not your child needs help in this arena.

For each of the items below, note how often you observe the specific behaviors described: consistently (C), often (O), infrequently (I), or never (N).

1. My child tends to be unaware of others' feelings.

   C   O   I   N

2. My child has difficulty sharing possessions.

   C   O   I   N

3. My child shows hostility toward siblings.

   C   O   I   N

4. My child has difficulty getting along with others.

   C   O   I   N

5. My child interrupts conversations.

   C   O   I   N

6. My child demands my full attention.

   C   O   I   N

7. My child damages things when upset.

   C   O   I   N

8. My child acts "spoiled."

   C   O   I   N

9. My child seeks more possessions.

   C   O   I   N

10. My child seeks control of the household.

    C   O   I   N

11. My child exhausts my patience.

    C   O   I   N

12. My child tattles on siblings.

    C   O   I   N

13. My child finds it hard to share.

    C   O   I   N

14. My child talks back to me with no respect.

    C   O   I   N

15. My child frustrates me.

    C   O   I   N

16. My child frightens me.

    C   O   I   N

17. My child wears me down.

    C   O   I   N

18. My child harms animals.

    C   O   I   N

19. My child starts fires.

    C   O   I   N

20. My child defies authorities and rules.

    C   O   I   N

Scoring

Add up the items for your overall score. For each time you marked a **C** (Consistently), give a score of 4; for each time you marked an **O** (Often), give a score of 2; and every time you marked an **I** (Infrequently), give a score of 1. Add the scores, and compare your total to the ranges below:

50–80 Your child needs to learn cooperative skills, or face lifelong problems forming loving relationships.

30–49 Your child may be confused about your relationship and the benefits of cooperation. You need to work out a daily program.

15–29 Your child is likely going through a typical learning period for cooperative relationships but seems to be on track.

0–14 You child seems to understand cooperation and is likely to develop healthy relationships.

There is no need for alarm if your child scored high in this assessment; however, it does mean that you need to begin a serious program to nurture cooperative attitudes and mutual support. You should come up with a daily plan for working on building a spirit of team work and cooperation while discouraging selfishness and antisocial behavior, using some of the ideas in this book.

THE COLLECTIVE GOOD

The irony in our inborn drive for self-preservation is that our greatest hope for long-term survival as a species lies in cooperation between individuals. After all, it takes two to tango, and even more to build a civilization and keep it going. It is also true that there are no leaders without followers. Our societies, organizations, governments, churches, states, and countries are built on cooperative effort; on individuals working for the common good; on men and women putting aside their selfish wants and needs for higher goals.

Legendary biologist, innovative thinker, and game theory pioneer Bill Hamilton once wrote a paper entitled *Geometry for the Selfish Herd*. It was based on the idea that herds of animals are arranged on the principle that each individual tries to maximize the chance that, if a predator appears at random and strikes at the nearest prey, *somebody else gets eaten.*

But Hamilton also came up with another theory that supports the concept of cooperation, not as a moral decision but as a natural survival instinct. Imagine a situation in which two gang members—Ratso and Fatso—are arrested and accused of breaking into a house to burglarize it. The penalty for this crime is $100 and/or a year in jail. Since there are no witnesses, they are interrogated separately, and each is offered freedom and a reward of $500 for squealing on the other. But their gang ups the ante by promising both a bonus of $300 if they keep quiet, which would force the police to release them. The other option would be for both Ratso and Fatso to blame each other, in which case both would go to jail and be fined instead of collecting any reward or bonus.

If they're driven purely by self-interest, you might expect that Ratso or Fatso would turn on the other because the squealer would get an extra $200. But then, Ratso is being shown the same options, and if he talks, Fatso goes to jail. The short-term solution would be for one of the gang members to squeal on the other, grab the $500 reward, and leave his buddy behind bars. That would be the self-centered, survivor approach.

But the wild card thrown in by Hamilton is "future consequences." What if Ratso and Fatso were told that if either of them turned on the other, the gang would take revenge on the squealer and his family? That would change the dynamic considerably, wouldn't it? Hamilton believed that over the long haul, certain cooperative behavior promotes the self-interest of the individual. He came up with an answer to a problem that had baffled even Charles Darwin. Our behavior begins to be determined by our future consequences of social, rather than personal, survival. After all, the survival of human beings has ultimately always rested on community support rather than individual strength.

Naturalists had long been puzzled by this conundrum: if organisms are inherently selfish, and dedicated to their own survival and reproduction, why do so many species seem to be willing to sacrifice for the good of others? Common examples of this include worker bees that take care of their queen's offspring rather than breeding their own, or auntie bees who sacrifice their own lives to defend the hive from intruders. Hamilton theorized that the bees view all members of the colony as essentially one organism, so they act unselfishly to preserve the colony as a whole. Although they appear to be unselfish in their sacrifice, they are actually behaving selfishly.

This form of survival instinct explains how our communities and cultures have evolved and endured. We realize we must cooperate and sometimes sacrifice individual freedoms so that our children and grandchildren will be able to carry on in a functioning society. The critical aspect of this involves taking the long-term view. When children see only the short-term, they tend to be self-centered because they don't understand that the short-term rewards will be followed by long-term consequences.

The principle of community sacrifice goes back to before recorded history; the role of the warrior has always been to place himself between the enemy and the community. Our religions have this central message as a primary place of honor among us.

Adults generally understand the long-term benefits of altruistic or unselfish behavior that benefits society as a whole. But children need to be taught the long-term view and the benefits of cooperation and selflessness. Too often, parents forget this and assume that their children are born as benevolent angels with generous hearts.

TEACHING COOPERATION

I've developed these guidelines for helping parents teach their children the cooperative and unselfish attitudes that are necessary for them to succeed in society.

- *There is always a reason for a behavior, and when that reason can be expressed in other ways, there is no more reason for destructive behavior.*

This is one of the most important principles in child psychology. Children act out for a reason. Your job is to figure it out. When you do, then you need to let your child know that you understand what is going on. That should stop your child's need to continually physically express his desire.

When Johnny throws a tantrum, it is safe to assume that he wants to get attention for some reason. The key is to ignore the behavior and focus on the message behind it. You should tell Johnny that you understand he wants attention. If you are right, Johnny will likely end the tantrum. You should take the opportunity to teach him how to get attention in a constructive way, but the critical thing is to show him that he doesn't have to turn into a screaming banshee to get attention.

I once worked as a juvenile probation officer, and my research in that field found that children who continually get into trouble often have problems expressing themselves in more acceptable ways. They don't know how to say what is on their minds, so they act out in frustration. The more stressed they are, the worse their behavior. But if we help them express themselves in constructive ways, they will do that. You also show that you truly care for them when you take the time to understand rather than to simply react.

• *Sympathy conveys pity and shame, not compassion.*

I came home from a particularly tough high school football practice one night and told my dad that I wanted to quit because my coaches hated me and would never give me a chance.

My dad listened, but he didn't give me the sympathy I was hoping for.

"Well, it sounds like you are having a tough time, so I guess you will have to show them they're wrong. You have done it before and you can do it this time too. I have faith in you. They'll come around once you prove yourself to them."

I wanted my dad to cuss out the coaches and tell me to go ahead and quit—or at least, that's what I thought I wanted. But his response was really what I needed to hear. He acknowledged my feelings, but he also let me know that he was there for me and that he believed in me. That is what every child needs to know. To give love, we must know we are loved. To care for others, we must know others care for us.

It is true that things will happen to your children that really are sad and unfair. You should respond with empathy and support, not sympathy, resentment, or bitterness toward external factors. I know, easier said than done. Like most parents, I have had to bite my tongue when I've seen my own children treated unfairly. But as a parent, your job is not to vent; it is to teach your child how to respond to adversity in a positive manner. What happens to us is often beyond our control. But we can control how we let it affect us, and how we respond.

- *Cooperation and love are the ultimate keys.*

Americans have long prized rugged individualism. Self-reliance is an attribute that should be encouraged. But you do your children and yourself a great disservice if you do not teach them the rewards of teamwork and cooperation. Praise and develop your child's unique talents and attributes, but help them see how their gifts can contribute to the greater good. It is a delicate balance at times. You should encourage your child's creativity and individuality. But even the most talented and brilliant people need to work with others to get the most out of their labors.

- *Preview/review is a requirement for learning loving relationships.*

I often recommend that parents hold strategy sessions with their children, just as coaches and military leaders do with their players and soldiers before going into action. It pays to sit down with your child and discuss any issues that are expected to arise, whether it is the impending arrival of a new sibling, the breakup of a marriage, or a move to a new home. By previewing what lies ahead, you can ease fears and anxieties, and avoid behavioral problems down the road.

It is always helpful and important for parents to discuss cooperative approaches to challenges their children are facing. Approach these discussions from the perspective of "What can we do to deal with it?" Lay the groundwork for strong bonds and open communication by letting your children know that their concerns are your concerns and that you are willing to help them devise strategies.

Although no parent ever wants to hear this, your kid is going to make mistakes—lots of them. We all do. Prepare yourself for it and be part of your child's future by working out ways to deal with them.

I also recommend reviewing how those strategies worked or didn't work after they've been implemented. If your daughter was nervous about a first date, it is wise to sit down afterward and talk about how it went. Even if it went well, you are opening the lines of communication for those times when something may go badly. It is also helpful to talk through disagreements or arguments and to review how they were resolved. Again, you are building a foundation for open communication and smoother resolutions in the future—when the stakes are likely to be much higher.

THE PLAN

Some parents and children can talk things through. Others bond better while engaged in physical activities. I recommend doing whatever works best for you and your children. Here are some proactive activities and exercises that I recommend as bond-builders for families.

Day 1: Ball in Play

Learn to play together. There will be many opportunities to learn to enjoy interactions. Consider scheduling a time in which you can play for at least thirty minutes.

When I played football, my teammates and I invented a pre-workout game in which we sat in a circle and batted a football back and forth, trying to keep it in the air as long as possible. It was fun and got us warmed up, but more important, it was a cooperative endeavor that built up a team spirit that carried through into the practice or game ahead.

Parents and children can do the same thing using their favorite sports as a setting. Some try to keep a tennis ball or ping-pong ball going over the net. Others do it with a volleyball or basketball. I've read that the world record for continuous play with a tennis ball is 6,001 returns. You can imagine the teamwork that required. I challenge your family to beat it!

Day 2: Cook a Meal

You might want to keep a fire extinguisher handy, or a pizza delivery service on speed dial, for this one. But inviting your children to prepare a meal can be a great way of bringing the family together in a collaborative effort. As a special reward, those purple-grape-jelly-and-egg omelets may live on in family lore for decades!

By the way, children from the age of four can and should participate in this fun. In this case all nutritional guides can be shelved, and only those foods that require appropriate skills in preparation should be considered.

The idea, of course, is to have fun while working toward a goal together, even if it is only macaroni and cheese sandwiches. Take turns as the Head Chef. It would be great to do it to celebrate a good grade, a successful season, a birthday, Earth Day, or a Wednesday. Make certain that everyone also participates in the cleanup. (Mothers always appreciate that.)

Day 3: Family Walks

My family had a tradition of doing this. In fact, some nights it seemed like all of Texas was out strolling to stay cool. Air-conditioning came along and turned us into couch potatoes. Video games and computers have turned our kids into shut-ins. With childhood obesity a growing concern, this family activity has all kinds of benefits.

Children tend to open up when engaged in activities with their parents. Be prepared to field all sorts of unexpected questions along the way. You might bone up on your nature notes so you can talk about the sun and the moon, why birds sing, or how frogs croak. Be willing to talk about unimportant things now, so your children will be open to talking when truly important things come up.

Day 4: Drumming

This is surprisingly good family or group therapy, though you might get dirty looks from the neighbors. Get together a selection of percussion instruments, including pots and pans, to give each family member something to beat on, and let one person set the rhythm. Keep it up for twenty minutes.

It may sound chaotic at first, but after five minutes, organized patterns will emerge. Research has shown that the drummers begin to have similar brain patterns, which enhances communal spirit, mutual understanding, and cooperation. Therapists have used drumming to quell antisocial behavior in gang members. It's increasingly acknowledged that this Native American tradition served more than ceremonial purposes.

Day 5: Positive Hot Seat

Positive feedback can heal wounded spirits and hurt feelings. Too often parents focus so much on what a child is doing wrong that they neglect this important fact. To make use of positive feedback, designate a time each week for the family to get together and put one person in the "hot seat" in the center of the room. One by one, take turns telling the person on the hot seat something positive. It could be something they've done, a talent they've expressed, or even a physical attribute. Think of it as putting coins in a bank account. The more you put in now, the more your child will have to draw out when it is needed.

Day 6: Pray for Each Other

Prayers come in many forms. If your family belongs to a church, you probably have some favorites. Even if you don't practice an established religion, there are benefits to expressing good feelings and caring intentions for each other.

Gather together one night a week and talk about your individual concerns, hopes, and dreams. Then take turns wishing for good outcomes for each other. Pray in the manner of your faith, or simply express good wishes and caring feelings for each member of the family. These sessions may feel awkward at first, but they can also produce incredible moments of intimacy and love.

Day 7: Puzzles and Games

My grandmother seemed to always have a puzzle going on a cardboard table in her living room. Family members were invited to work on it as they walked by, or to sit down and get serious about it. It was an informal family ritual, but I can still remember being praised for fitting pieces together. It made me feel like I was contributing to a family project. I was young, but I was part of an adult undertaking. Children benefit from such feelings. Invite yours to join in and encourage them as they participate in fun family projects, whether it is putting a puzzle together, painting a room, or building a snowman.

Days 8–10

Have a meeting and decide which of the previous exercises meant the most to you. Find a way to decide on three of them, or create new ones for yourselves. Complete the exercises as planned.

PROACTIVE PARENTING

Often parents come to me for help, saying, "I was hoping my child would just grow out of this." That is a dangerous and risky form of parenting, if it even deserves that title. It is your responsibility as a parent to get actively engaged in nurturing, shaping, teaching, and guiding your children. This requires you to be proactive rather than reactive. The investment of time and love that you make in their childhood will pay benefits throughout your lifetime and theirs. Your child, like all children, is instinctively selfish. You must teach cooperation and collaboration. And you must serve as an example and role model. It may not always be easy, but it doesn't have to be painful either. And it will not always go according to your plans. I have always said, "If you want to see God laugh, tell Him your plans."

Don't let that scare you. If you do your job as a parent, your child will surprise you in wonderful and loving ways.

4

Natural Healing Powers

This is the third segment in the 90-day program. You should allot ten days, including two weekends, to complete this segment. In this chapter, you will learn to use natural, mental, and sensory tools, including smell, touch, and taste, to build the bonds of love between you and your child.

There are few things more heart-wrenching than watching desperate parents struggle to bond with their children. It's not that parents don't try. Nobody sets out to be a lousy mom or dad, but there are many out there who simply don't know what they don't know.

Most parents want to have loving bonds with their children. They aspire to create the perfect Hollywood version of a happy family. But it takes more than good intentions to develop loving, lasting bonds, and many parents simply don't have the skills or the tools to get the job done.

Some try very hard. I've had parents come to me spilling over with newly acquired knowledge of behavioral modification techniques that they hope will build the bonds they so dearly want. Yet there are far simpler and potentially more effective tools that come more naturally and work more powerfully. Some lie beneath their noses and within their olfactory systems!

I'm speaking from years of experience not only as a family counselor, but also from my research and practice in the field of pain control at Southwestern Medical School in Dallas, and at Stanford University Medical School. Medical science is just beginning to grasp the powers of physical healing that lie within each of us. I also have observed and put to practical use the innate spiritual and emotional healing tools we possess. As doctors and patients, we have come to rely so much on pills, potions, and intellectual gymnastics in our search for quick cures that we have tended to overlook the natural methods of healing used by our earliest civilizations.

My scientific research in this arena was driven by the suffering of children in horrific pain. Too many times, I watched young patients and their parents in anguish during spinal taps, blood tests, or other procedures. I've seen some hospitals call out four or five staff members to hold down a thrashing child driven mad with pain, and I've seen children needlessly drugged and dangerously sedated. I knew there had to be better ways, and I found them without great difficulty, simply by opening my mind to alternative approaches and then applying modern scientific methods of investigation to test their effectiveness.

One of my earliest encounters with natural healing occurred within the Taos Pueblo in New Mexico. I'd gone there to study shamanic healing methods practiced by spiritual leaders. I was fascinated by the methods of a woman who specialized in working with children. She had an incredibly calming presence, radiating loving concern and empathy as she soothed screaming babies by gently massaging them and singing softly. No needles, knives, or narcotics were deployed. This natural healer instead used her own biological and emotional powers to trigger those within each child she encountered.

Every doctor, nurse, and medical professional who deals with sick children and their families has heard parents remark that the one blessing to emerge from traumatic illness is the strengthening of familial bonds. It is a common phenomenon. We come together as a natural response to crisis because we have the power to soothe and even heal each other. It is part of our nature as social beings.

Great physical, emotional, and spiritual healers within the medical establishment and outside it find ways to tap and trigger those innate recuperative and restorative resources. In this chapter, you will survey a range of nonverbal techniques for healing, soothing, and restoring your emotional bonds with your children. Many of them have come out of folk customs and nontraditional healing, but all have proven scientific validity. They are "magic" only in the way that our biological, emotional, and spiritual compositions are magical. Is a beating heart magical?

SCIENCE OF LOVE

The magic is rooted in our physiology. We are wondrous creations, and it is likely that we operate well below our capacities on many levels. Scientific understanding of what lies within us grows exponentially day to day. We do know that caring and cooperative behaviors are driven by hormones from deep within the brain's cortex, beyond human consciousness. Two hormones in particular appear to be responsible for triggering altruistic actions: oxytocin and vasopressin. Researchers have found those hormones present in high amounts when examining test subjects involved in intimate relationships.

When women have sex, and also when they give birth to and nurture their children, the oxytocin receptors in the brain are fired up on brain scans like the skies on the Fourth of July. This intense response occurs near the center of the brain in females and slightly off to the side in males during emotional peaks. These regions release high levels of dopamine, the brain's supercharger, which excites the mind to increased levels of exhilaration and imagination. Too much dopamine can overstimulate the brain and cause schizophrenia.

Low levels of dopamine in some areas of the brain are thought to trigger Parkinson's.

During emotional peaks some regions of the brain are deactivated, including those that guide clear thinking and focus attention and memory. All of these interactions serve to produce very positive feelings. You might know it as the "floating sensation" experienced at the height of passion, and in the thrall of love. There is science to back up the concept of being "blinded by love," since your ability to think clearly is slowed by the hormones released. One of my favorite descriptions for this state of mind is offered up in the Disney classic *Bambi,* when spring arrives and love-struck creatures are said to be "twitterpated."

The sensation of loving and being loved is very much part of the human experience—as well as the Bambi and Thumper experience—and it undoubtedly serves as a survival mechanism of some sort. It is experienced in different, but equally powerful, forms between parents and children, grandparents and grandchildren, long-term friends, and others who have loving relationships. The triggers for these natural feelings of closeness are nonverbal forms of communication that bring into play our senses of smell, touch, and taste too.

MAKING SCENTS

My mother often cooked beans with gobs of bacon, so as a very young child, I associated her with that strong odor. To this day, I can't smell beans and bacon without thinking of her. We tend to overlook or underestimate the power that scents have in our interactions, yet the nerve connections between the "smell centers" in your brain are five times those in the brain's vision center.

The human scents we detect are called pheromones, airborne particles that we are only now beginning to understand in terms of their impact on human behavior. We do know that pheromones are given off by humans and other mammals during moments of sexual arousal and heightened anxiety and fear. Insects, such as mosquitoes and bees, appear to react to fear pheromones as well.

Pat Owen, a psychologist and scientist, and I conducted a study of human pheromones and how they reflect and impact emotional states. We asked four female college students to imagine three separate situations in which they would feel stressed, sexually aroused, and deeply relaxed. We took swab samples from each student's armpit after each imagined scenario. We then placed the swab samples in test tubes. Next, we asked ten male college students to smell the test tubes and then tell us what images came to mind. They had no idea what was in them. There were high correlations between the images that came to mind for the men and the situations the women had imagined before the swabs were taken. The highest correlations were for relaxed states, which surprised us. We suspected that humans could sense stress, sexual arousal, and calm, but we were surprised at how simply imagining those scenarios proved so effective in triggering pheromones.

Scientists have established that humans give off detectable odors that signal:

- Love and nurturing
- Stress
- Fear
- Anger
- Relaxation and peace
- Hunger
- Death

Pheromones and scents have tremendous roles repairing or creating distance in the bonds between parents and children. Pheromones—or the inability to detect them—can be responsible for disaffection between parent and child. Children can detect, better than adults can, the instant a mother changes attitude toward them. More critical, they can sense the loss of affection and positive feelings more quickly than they could through visual or voice interactions.

Even in animal studies, when rat babies had their smell detectors intentionally muted, they became disoriented to the mothers' caring, and highly stressed. The scents of caring are vital parts of the bonding process. One remarkable implication of this fact is that, by masking our pheromones with perfumes, we might be censoring important emotional messages, and interfering with bonding.

Even conflicts between parents and children can be linked to one giving off scents that repel the other. It's been reported, for example, that when girls reach puberty, they are repelled by pheromones given off by their fathers, which may be nature's way of discouraging inbreeding. Mothers and fathers often smell their babies and children instinctively. A parent with a poor sense of smell could have problems bonding because he can't pick up on his child's scent. Parents and children who have failed to bond may have a conflict that only the nose knows.

Just as your heart responds to your emotional states by beating more rapidly or slowly, your sweat glands give off odors that reflect emotional states. It might also be helpful to consciously seek to put out calming scents rather than those associated with fear or anxiety when attempting to build bonds with your child. You can do this, much as the female students in our tests did, by envisioning scenarios or situations that will trigger the pheromones and odors associated with the desired emotions. It might also be helpful to get in a relaxed position and to speak in soothing tones while listening to calming music.

You don't have to do it all yourself when it comes to producing scents, though. Home remedies and folk medicine have long touted the value of the aromas of certain plants and their essential oils.

There is a booming market in aromatherapy, with hundreds of Web sites offering plant oils that are alleged to promote psychological and physical well-being. Native American shamans believed in the healing powers of mesquite and sage. Cinnamon, pumpkin, and vanilla scents have been used as natural mood enhancers to prompt soothing and relaxed states of mind. Honeysuckle has been promoted as a scent that encourages a forgiving mood, and aspen is said to ease anxiety.

There are scores of companies that offer tinctures of herbs, plants, and flowers for a variety of ailments or as mood enhancers. There also are candle makers who infuse these oils into their products. I have tried some of the aromatherapy scents on page 77, and while I can't provide much scientific proof, there have been instances when they seemed to promote the desired healing moods. There is certainly no evidence that aromatherapy has ever caused harm.

I generally expose individuals to the smell and then explain what each odor has the capacity to do. Parents have told me that their children's attitudes toward them improve if they rub certain of these essences on their skin.

HEALING TOUCH

In the late 1960s I worked for the Arkansas Rehabilitation Center. My job was to help disabled individuals regain their independence and, if possible, find gainful employment. This hospital also offered special services for the mentally handicapped and people with emotional disorders. One of our young clients, Delores, ten, had been institutionalized for two years due to severe, immobilizing depression. Nothing appeared to help her. Delores was stuck in the gates of hell, beyond help of even strong medications. She was all but paralyzed, moving only when assisted. She rarely spoke except to say "Thank you" or "No, sir." Though she was not yet a teenager, she

TABLE 1

Common Aromatherapeutic Remedies

Scent	Reputed Effect
Agrimony	Promotes expression of concerns
Aspen	Eases relationship anxiety
Beech	Lowers criticalness
Centaury	Focuses on boundaries of self
Cerato	Alleviates PMS
Cherry plum	Calms relationship concerns
Chicory	Eases possessiveness
Clematis	Helps concentration
Crab apple	Eases painful memories
Elm	Builds confidence
Ginseng	Relieves mild depression
Heather	Treats self-absorption
Holly	Alleviates envy and suspiciousness
Honeysuckle	Eases hurtful memories
Impatiens	Promotes patience
Larch	Boosts self-esteem
Mustard	Eases depression
Oak	Builds resolve
Olive	Builds vitality in relationships
Pine	Helps in guilt reduction
Red chestnut	Reduces worries
Star of Bethlehem	Eases child trauma
Walnut	Helps adaptation to changes
Water violet	Eases stubbornness
White chestnut	Promotes mental health
Wild oak	Reduces ambivalence, strengthens purpose
Wild rose	Enhances intimacy
Willow	Eases bitterness

walked with the stooped shoulders and shuffled gait of a ninety-year-old woman. Delores likely would never have changed her clothes if the other patients had not helped her. The only thing that seemed to strike a hopeful spark was her brown teddy bear, which she doted on.

Delores had lost her parents and two younger sisters in a car crash two years before I met her. The tragedy transformed her from a smart and lively ten-year-old to this sad shell of a human. None of our standard treatments for depression seemed to work. She responded to our treatment questions with a series of grunts and gestures. Finally, I decided to improvise.

I'd done some research in therapeutic massage, and I thought it might be helpful in this case. This technique is simply a soothing touch in long strokes down the back and neck muscles, with instructions to breathe and relax to the touch. This is not unlike the touching method commonly used by mothers the world over, with the addition of comforting sounds and music. (Of course, in science we have to sanitize any natural loving behavior with a clinical name.)

Therapeutic massage can relax a child and decrease anxiety, but it also can enhance energy by releasing stress and creating a cascade of endorphins (neurotransmitters produced by the body to inhibit pain and stress messaging to the brain). It can also prompt a release of fear and enhance the connections to other human beings.

Delores had shied away from human contact since entering our hospital because of previous failures in alleviating the pain in her arms and legs. She was extremely depressed. Muscle spasms ran down her back whenever she tried to move. She was in a chronic, stagnant, hopeless condition. I hoped to break through her pain by reaching out to her. I had her recline facedown on a massage table with a physical therapist seated at her head to monitor her responses and to reassure her. I gently placed my hands on the small of her back, and I felt her shudder. It may have been my imagination, as emotions were running high for all of us, but it seemed as though an aching sensation ran through my hands. I wanted to believe that her pain and suffering were draining out through me.

My touch seemed to have an impact on the child. She began to weep and then sob. At first, I feared I was scaring her or making her condition worse, but the therapist heard her mutter a few words, and then she began to speak more than we'd ever heard. Delores talked nonstop for another hour, hardly allowing time for the therapist to respond. Finally, as our session came to an end, she hopped off the table and literally danced out of the room. We continued these touch therapy sessions over six days, with the therapist eventually taking charge of Delores's treatment. A month later, Delores left the hospital and returned to school and a normal life. She eventually graduated with honors and went on to college.

HEALING HANDS

There are three basic elements to touch therapy: location of the turmoil or pain in the body, nature of the touch, and the healer's imagery.

Location of Turmoil

Based on my clinical experiences and training in bioenergetics (a treatment philosophy founded by Wilhelm Reich in which emotions are thought to be stored in muscles and organs), I've found that stress is often focused in specific areas of the body where you would typically expect to feel "knotted up." Those who carry a lot of responsibility and feel burdened often report pain in their shoulders, neck, and lower back.

I have drawn a topology of these body sites to help guide your treatments. If you feel the tension, you might ask your child if she is feeling similar pains. This chart will give you clues as to how your child is feeling, and what the causes might be.

Body Topology Map of Stress Areas

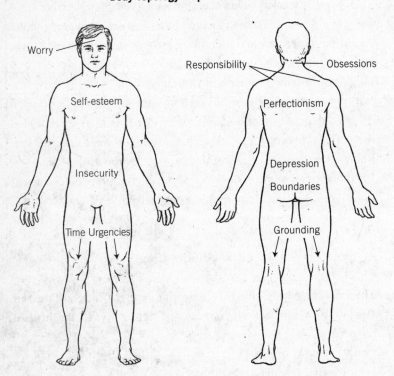

You can focus the massage therapy on certain areas of the body, depending on your child's emotional state. Depression often is treated by working the lower back area. A child who feels overwhelmed should be treated at the back of the head and in the upper neck region. Keep in mind that each child is different, so this is a very intuitive process. Use my map as a guide, but be willing to try other approaches. The most important thing is to touch and hug your child in appropriate ways in order to create a nurturing relationship.

Remember, by reaching out even in good times, you throw open the door for your child to come to you in troubled times. I recently treated a seven-year-old gymnast for muscle spasms related to stress from competition. We resolved her pain, but the child got so much mental and emotional relief from the massage therapy that I trained her mother to use it as a bonding tool.

The most preferred touch technique is to use slow, smooth strokes of your hands, creating a comforting pace for relaxing. Deep massage can be used, but this can be painful at times. When you practice massage therapies, you nurture loving bonds with your child both physically and emotionally.

While sitting or standing, hold your hands in front of you with your palms facing each other, about one inch apart. Close your eyes so you can concentrate totally on the sensations in your hands, especially the palms. Begin to vary the distance between the palms of your hands, and see if you can detect a sense of heat or tingling feelings in your palms. If so, use your relaxation breathing or positive imagery to enhance that sensation. It is this sensation that is described as your "life force," your "qi," or your "chi."

PROCEED WITH CAUTION

Some parents can simply sense when their children need hugs and caresses. These sensitive folks are blessed with instinctive and empathetic gifts of touch. But we all have the ability to reach out to our children and convey our love by touching them. Think of it as a way to share your life force, your energy, and your feelings for your child. I coach parents to think positive and loving thoughts when they reach out to their children with hugs and caresses.

There is healing power in the human touch, but it is also tricky territory because of potential abuse by quacks and predators. It's sad that such concerns have discouraged use of this therapy. Certainly massage therapy is widely recognized as a legitimate method for treating physical and emotional problems. Numerous theories, including those behind acupressure, hold that the body possesses energy fields that when disrupted cause emotional and physiological disharmony, but with the administration of touch those energy fields are stabilized.

There is not a lot of solid science to support these theories, but there is a large body of anecdotal evidence. The U.S. Defense Department funded a study of the effects of therapeutic touch, and found that anxiety and perceptions of pain were lower for the touched patients than the control group of patients who did not receive touch therapy. Other studies have been performed with mixed results.

Most of the natural healers who specialize in treating children use touch as a cornerstone. Orphaned children and even animals and plants have shown significant improvement in health from therapeutic touch.

Insurance companies still don't provide coverage for touch therapies as a general rule, but there may come a time when even those conservative institutions see the light. The challenges to widespread acceptance include the vast cultural differences when it comes to touching. For some, a hug is a traditional sign of long-term commitment. For others, a hug between strangers is considered an invasion of privacy, even an insult. President Bush's attempt to massage the shoulders of German chancellor Angela Merkel was seen over the world as a major diplomatic faux pas; it probably said more about the cultural differences between gregarious Texans and certain aloof Germans. Still, the resulting controversy illustrates that you have to be very careful whom you touch and how you touch them, even if your intentions are to heal.

FOOD FOR LOVE

Like the senses of smell and touch, our sense of taste has a role in familial bonding. Throughout human history and across diverse cultures, the practice of "breaking bread" at family meals has served as a bonding experience. If you doubt the bonding power of shared meals, food, and taste, ask yourself, How many times have I heard adults express warm affection and fond memories for the home-cooked meals of their childhoods? I can easily bring smiles to someone's face by asking about his mother's fried chicken or sweet potato pie, or her father's grilled steaks or barbecued ribs, or the grandmother's chocolate chip cookies or homemade fudge.

Your bonds with your child can be enhanced by tapping the sense of taste, or they can be strained, perhaps even broken, when emotional traps are placed around the table. Consider the prominent role that shared meals have played across most cultures. Around the world, we gather to eat as we celebrate holidays and major events such as weddings, christenings, burials, birthdays, graduations, and sports or academic accomplishments. And when sociologists and social commentators lament the disintegration of families, how often do they cite as an example the fact that parents and children don't sit down for family suppers as often as they once did?

Consider too the emotional debate over breast-feeding. Advocates believe that it is essential for the bonding of mothers and their children. Some studies have shown that breast-fed babies are less anxious than those who are bottle-fed by their mothers. But many mothers who don't breast-feed are equally adamant that their methods for providing nourishment are every bit as nurturing. Both sides feel that powerful bonding takes place during the feeding process. And there is ample evidence that when it is disrupted, relationship damage can result.

Josh and his mother, Andrea, came to me for help when the boy was just three years old. His mother was concerned that he did not seem to connect with his parents or other people. He was detached and uninterested in human contact. Andrea said that her relationship with her son had been strained from the very beginning because he could not digest her breast milk. When she breast-fed him, Josh became colicky and irritable. He developed diarrhea and became severely dehydrated. That medical emergency proved so stressful that Andrea constantly fretted over the boy's eating habits. It did not help that Josh was small and underweight for his age group. He also seemed to have impaired development in his communication skills. By the age of three, he still communicated mostly in grunts and gestures.

I found Josh to be well behaved but distant. He acknowledged my presence but was not inclined to interact unless I pushed it, preferring to play alone with his blocks. To encourage interaction, I brought out my secret weapon for capturing the attention of disinterested children—Wheaties, the vaunted "breakfast of champions." (I'm hoping to get my picture on the box one of these days, can you tell?) General Mills doesn't need my endorsement, but I have found that Wheaties is my "meal of power" and makes for a healthy play food that is nourishing.

Josh responded like a champ to my Wheaties gambit. He popped the first one I offered into his mouth and then eagerly engaged in a game of "Which hand has the Wheaties?" Using his finger to point, he guessed wrong the first time, but picked the right hand the next try. That provoked a laugh, and his first words heard by his mother: "You are funny. I like this game."

Over the course of our next four meetings, I used other tasty treats to draw out Josh. We shared peanut butter on wafers, wheat cookies, raisins, and frozen grapes. Establishing a bond with food proved to work well for me, but it required a good six months using the same methods to heal his bonds with his parents.

Naturally the parents quickly learned the power of food as a reinforcement to social connections. One caution is that sugar levels need to be controlled so other reinforcers can develop, but food does serve as a very powerful link in relationships.

MATTERS OF TASTE

Josh's case illustrates the power of taste as a bonding force and as a powerful incentive in human behavior. The more we like something, the more we are willing to pay for it. Consider the prices demanded for fine chocolates or the best brands and vintages of wine. When sugar cane was introduced as a treat for the European elite in the 1800s, it was hailed as "white gold" because of the sweet prices they were willing to pay for it.

Our craving for certain tastes is usually tied to a physiological or emotional need. We crave salt when our bodies sense an electrolyte imbalance. People who have gone without food for days often report a craving for foods rich in protein. Those suffering from depression often experience a craving for chocolate, which has been shown to trigger chemical reactions in the body that create more pleasurable states.

THE INVISIBLE GLUE FOR BONDING

When I built a swing set recently for my younger children with my father-in-law, we discovered in the early hours that this was not going to be a one-day job. The instructions were incomprehensible. None of the thousands of boards and bolts had labels on them. We called this the "mystery project," because we had no idea what it would look like.

When we finally sorted out enough pieces to get started, the first board was screwed to another. My father-in-law said: "This is the first step and the most important one for all mankind." We laughed at the announcement as if we had started the staging for landing on the moon, but both of us knew that as simple as the task was, it laid the groundwork for everything else we would do. It had to be right.

So it is with taking the first step toward building a love bond with your child. We always want to get to the end result, but love has to be patient and consistent. The *intention* to bond is actually more important than the action. Focusing on creating a loving scent, touching your child, or making nurturing food are *avenues* for developing the love connection.

Once I instructed a father to use touch as a means of conveying love to his child, and he hobbled into the office the next week with a brace around his neck. He looked miserable. He explained that he was so intent on rubbing his child's back that he developed inflammation in his own neck and back after three hours. He was disappointed that his efforts had not yielded a single positive response. It was clear that he had followed my suggestions, but he'd failed to get the emotional context. Instead of focusing on the touch technique itself, I told him to imagine what feelings he wanted to convey while he touched his child. He had a very different response when he rubbed his child's back with those feelings in mind. Initially, he was like a man expecting a woman to fall in love with him simply because he brought flowers on a date.

I offer these methods for building bonds because they have been used for generations. Our bodies and minds recognize them as loving acts, but without emotional involvement, there is nothing. Be conscious of each part of the act in using sensory pathways. When you are touching a child, be aware of your touch and what you want it to mean. When you feed a child, be aware of the nurturing feelings you want to convey. When you are using smell, be attuned to its power and intimacy.

We don't heal bonds simply by taking the right actions. It takes emotional commitment. A touch at the right time can change the world. A single taste can open a world of dreams and passion. It is the small but loving behavior that burrows into the consciousness and awakens hearts to another.

THE PLAN

The exercises for this ten-day plan are summarized below. As in the development of any skill, consider the timing as a guide but not a rule. Some exercises will be more relevant to one particular person than others.

Days 1–2

Experiment with different scents in your home and observe their effects on your family's emotions. For example, have your favorite flowers or scented candles present at specific times of the day (mornings and evenings) to see if your children are more relaxed or cheerful. You could even use some Bach flower remedies for their purported uses (alleviation of stress, relief of depression, higher concentration, etc.).

Day 3

While putting your child to bed, give hugs and rub the child's shoulders, back, and neck to feel for any tension. Send positive human energy to your child, without speaking. Note how quickly the child relaxes and begins to feel better. You don't have to spend a lot of time doing this, but try to leave your child in a relaxed and restful state.

Day 4

If your child is irritated or upset, reach out and comfort by massaging the "webs" between fingers and toes in a calming way. These are very sensitive areas, and massaging them triggers the release of soothing chemicals in the brain. Talk soothingly and reassuringly as you do this.

Day 5

Children often enjoy giving their parents back rubs. Some families make a game of it, challenging the kids to "draw pictures" on the parent's back with their fingers, which the parents then try to guess. This is a very simple and fun way to bond through touch. It helps build trust and adds a very important form of communication.

Day 6

Set aside one meal a day in which bonding with your child or children is a specific goal. Go out or eat in, but focus on healthy foods that your child likes, and center the conversations on the child's interests. Make it relaxed and fun. Provide special treats and surprises.

Day 7

Making a meal together can be as great a bonding experience as eating together, but in this exercise make a rule that everyone has to use their hands instead of using utensils. It will get messy real quick, and I don't advise doing it when the boss is over, but a change in eating behavior based on the fun of eating can create memorable experiences. Even parents will be clumsy, and making a meal will become a different experience.

Day 8

Pick a slow time at the grocery store. Use the hunting-gathering experience to bond. Let your child have a say in the selection, but use the outing to educate your child on why you pick certain foods as healthier than others. Stress the importance of eating foods that give the child "go-power" for things he enjoys, such as sports, games, and other activities.

Day 9

Plant a small garden with your child to teach her about the source of fruits and vegetables. Your child's interest in healthy and natural foods will be nurtured and relationship bonds enhanced as together you watch seeds, bulbs, and cuttings grow into food that you can then prepare and eat together.

Day 10

Telling your children you love them and listening to them with patience and understanding is a great way to strengthen the bonds between you. But in addition to vocal communication, you need to communicate your love as well. I recommend at least one hundred hugs a day per child, and at least that many for parents. I'll even write you a prescription for it, if that helps remind you. I am a proud believer in the Warm Fuzzies School of Therapy for Children. In fact, I offer the following fable to children as well as parents in my clinic. (I don't know the original author, but I have added my own touches to it.) Read this story to your children:

Many years ago, before there was time or war, the primary way people kept alive was through warm fuzzies. Warm fuzzies were exchanged by touching and exchanging positive energies. When you walked away from a warm fuzzies encounter, you felt good and energized. Everyone was happy because warm fuzzies were plentiful and free.

But one day a very selfish individual, dressed in a strange uniform, showed up with a product called "cold pricklies," and explained that warm fuzzies were being limited by the government, and that the only substitutes were cold pricklies. Cold pricklies would not feel good, but they would keep you alive. The individual explained that everyone had only a limited number of warm fuzzies they were born with, and when they ran out, they had nothing of value for another.

Many people believed this report, and they scurried to build up a supply of cold pricklies, while conserving their remaining warm fuzzies. This caused a warm fuzzies deficit, and a black market in them bloomed. Lawsuits ensued.

Soon, people began to die from warm fuzzy deprivation. Counterfeit warm fuzzies were put into circulation despite penalties of ten years in jail for their use.

One day a kind and spiritual person came forth and explained that no one ever truly runs out of warm fuzzies, and the more you share, the more you have. The world rejoiced, but to this day certain uninformed people are still giving cold pricklies. They need to be educated to the fact that warm fuzzies are free, but have to be handled with care and trust.

After you have read the story, discuss what "warm fuzzies" are in real life. They are expressions of love and support, and for each person they are different. For me they are warm touches and hugs. For others, they might be kind behaviors, such as saying, "I love you," or giving a pat on the back with assuring words of encouragement. There are also ways of expressing your love through creating personal artwork, like cards and letters that show how much you care. Gifts of flowers and singing songs of care are on the list.

Require that everyone share what they perceive as warm fuzzies and make an agreement among everyone to give at least twenty fuzzies per day. There is also the requirement that if any one of you needs a warm fuzzy, you have to ask for it aloud.

REACHING OUT

In this chapter you are asked to reach out with a clear intention of touching and expressing yourself to your child. You are also asked to change habits of expressions of care. We all get too busy to show positive bonding because we are so focused on what we "need to do." Make the clear decision to switch your day up and demand of yourself some additional priorities. You need to find ways to remind yourself that today and every day from now, some of those waking hours will be spent on giving some of those warm fuzzies to your child, as well as receiving a few along the way. I promise you some major rewards.

5

Bonding beyond Words

This is the fourth segment in the 90-day program. Listening skills and body language are the tools of communication explored in this chapter. You should count on taking ten days, including two weekends, to complete this segment.

The ability to form lasting, loving bonds with our children is critical to their mental, physical, and spiritual health—and to ours too. But our best efforts to form those bonds can be thwarted or blocked by physiological and/or emotional problems. We found this to be the case in our treatment of Darin, a ten-year-old who came to my clinic labeled with a disturbing batch of diagnoses that included Asperger's syndrome, autism, ADHD, obsessive-compulsive disorder, bipolar disorder, severe depression, and a wide range of personality disorders. The files on him claimed he was hostile, uncooperative, disrespectful, inattentive, hot-tempered, and impulsive, among other things.

Darin had two sisters (three and five years older) who treated him like their spoiled child. He dominated them and his parents, causing resentment from the sisters. Even when the oldest daughter had a big soccer game, her parents could not attend because Darin created a crisis that kept them home. Yet for the most part Darin refused to interact with family members or to take part in their activities. He kept to himself unless he needed to turn on the charm to get what he wanted.

Darin's behavior was erratic, which led to all of the diagnoses handed out by his doctors. None was ever discarded, which says more about the inherent dangers of our medical system than it does about this boy's mental and physical health. Darin had also been placed on an alarming number of antidepressants, brain stimulants, antianxiety drugs, and sleep medications. Yet nothing seemed to work.

The boy continued to act out regularly, but when I interviewed him I saw little evidence of the monster portrayed in his records. He was an averaged-sized boy, about five feet tall, with short-cropped blond hair, good muscular development, and an athlete's frame. In our first meeting, he wore jeans and a dirty T-shirt. His grandmother, who brought him in, apologized by saying that it was impossible for Darin to stay clean.

My first impression was that he might have a form of autism or epilepsy, except that he could be quite personable and engaging, especially when he talked about his interests. He spoke with intelligence and considerable charm even while noting that he really didn't want to be at the clinic. Darin was alert and curious about his surroundings, but he had a skittish, nervous manner. It struck me immediately that he avoided eye contact; in fact, he never even looked at my face.

Darin had some awful habits that tended to isolate him socially. He could seem rude, selfish, and demanding, but he wasn't really a bad kid. He just lacked some very basic socialization tools.

Intrigued, I set up a battery of tests, beginning with a brain scan. Most kids balk or even refuse to put on the scary-looking cap with electrodes taped to their scalp, but Darin didn't raise any objections. During the testing process, we did determine that this boy had considerable difficulty concentrating. We homed in on that and discovered that it appeared to be related to visual problems. Darin

The essential features of Asperger's disorder are severe and sustained impairment in social interaction and the development of restricted, repetitive patterns of behavior, interests, and activities. The disturbance must cause clinically significant impairment to social, occupational, or other important areas of functioning. In contrast to Autistic Disorder, there are no clinically significant delays or deviance in language acquisition . . . although more subtle aspects of social communication . . . may be affected. (DSM-IV-TR, 2000)

struggled to bring his eyes into focus. He could see well once he adjusted his eyes, but they did not work well together. When we asked him to shift his focus from a figure on the wall to a sheet of paper, it took him much longer than it should have. We also found Darin to be extremely anxious. Even when he claimed to be relaxed, his breathing rate was 26 respirations a minute, which is within the range for hyperventilation. At that breathing rate, there is an imbalance in oxygen and carbon dioxide levels, which makes it difficult for the brain to process information.

Once we looked at his test results, we began to understand why Darin had behavioral issues. It appeared that many of them could be traced to his impaired visual skills. Darin's difficulty focusing his eyes for extended periods resulted in an inability to study the facial features of others. He could not "read" facial cues normally. As a result, he couldn't pick up on the emotions of others until he got verbal cues, which usually were expressed later, if at all. The poor kid was stressed because he was always playing catch-up. He had a real desire to please others, but he wasn't getting all the information he needed to respond to them.

We addressed his problems by giving him exercises and techniques to improve his ability to focus his eyes. Within two weeks, he learned to focus normally. Then we gave him special training in recognizing facial expressions and the emotions associated with them. We had him hang the Feelings Chart (C. J. Lawlis, 2006) reproduced on page 96, which shows a range of expressions and the emotions they reflect, on his family's refrigerator. He responded eagerly, but it took a lot of training to get him to read faces for emotional cues.

Darin's behavior improved dramatically once he got the hang of it. He learned to respond to facial cues, and the positive reinforcement eased his nervous temperament. As part of his advanced training, we gave Darin a course designed to teach salespeople how to read facial and body cues. He became such a master at it that his teachers worried he might become manipulative of other students, particularly girls. It seemed we had done our job a little too well.

The real magic was in Darin's relationships with his family. They'd always thought he was autistic, as described by the school, and had become accustomed to meager interpersonal interactions with him. It was obvious that they had no idea what kind of person he was, or what he needed from them. After a few months of work, they were amazed by his willingness to follow directions and requests. It appeared that he discovered the joy of being praised for accommodating others, and he became very charming.

With greater understanding of the feelings of people around him, Darin began to enjoy conversations and discovering others' personalities. It was as if a new child had been born, and this kid was really interesting. There was a sense of celebration, of breakthrough; this unresponsive child could be a gift for everyone.

MINDSIGHT

Darin's behavioral problems were caused by his lack of *mindsight*—the ability to read and react to the emotions of others. I've found that mindsight is critical to forming bonds and relationships. The

Angry

Anxious

Ashamed

Confident

Confused

Disgusted

Depressed

Frightened

Guilty

Enraged

Happy

Exhausted

Jealous

Hopeful

Frustrated

Lonely

Overwhelmed

Shy

Sad

Suspicious

Bored

Relaxed

Energetic

Excited

Feelings (*C. J. Lawlis*)

lack of it is a definite social handicap, and it is often first noticed when children have difficulty bonding with those they should be closest to—their parents and other family members.

Have you ever noticed how children intently study the faces of their parents? Babies and toddlers don't have language skills, so they have to develop the ability to read facial expressions and to communicate through their own nonverbal cues; thus, the cries, the screams, and the cuddly coos. When vision problems interfere with reading facial cues, children can become frustrated and confused, resulting in antisocial issues. That is the reason Darin had problems. He could not read or respond to facial expressions, which frustrated him and caused him to act out in other ways.

Assessing Your Child's Mindsight

Perhaps your loving bonds with your child have not developed or have been lost because of physiological challenges like those Darin experienced. I've provided this assessment exercise to help you determine if that is the case.

For each description answer either always (A), sometimes (S), rarely (R), or never (N) present.

1. My child does not look into my eyes when we talk.

   A   S   R   N

2. My child has difficulty reading my unspoken emotions.

   A   S   R   N

3. My child does not hang out with friends.

   A   S   R   N

4. My child becomes distracted in conversations.

   A   S   R   N

5. My child seems preoccupied and detached.

   A   S   R   N

6. My child blurts out unrelated ideas during conversations.

   A   S   R   N

7. My child gets nervous during social interactions.

   A   S   R   N

8. My child expresses feelings of victimization.

   A   S   R   N

9. My child has fantasy friends or romances.

   A   S   R   N

10. My child prefers to be alone.

   A   S   R   N

Scoring

For each A marked, give a credit of 3; for each S marked, give a credit of 2; and for each R marked, give a credit of 1. Add up all the credits for a total score in a range between 0 and 30. If your total score is greater than 9, there is indication that your child has poorly developed mindsight. If the score is greater than 15, there is definitely a need to consider that your child has deficits in mindsight that may contribute to behavior problems.

MINDSIGHT TRAINING

The ability to read and react to the emotional states of others is an important socialization and communication skill. The lack of mindsight can contribute to a wide range of behavioral problems in both children and adults. These exercises can help improve your child's mindsight.

1. Encourage the child and the family to label the facial expressions for emotion every day on the Feelings Chart on page 96.
2. As the child identifies each feeling and the face associated with it, ask: "What makes you feel this way? How does it happen that you begin to feel this way? What do you do when you feel this way?"
3. Have all the family members describe their feeling states and how things and events affect their feelings.
4. Have a family or group discussion on nonverbal cues. Talk about each other's cues and what each means.
5. Tell your child to gaze into a person's eyes and then to describe what that person is feeling.
6. Discuss other nonverbal cues, such as tone of voice, body posture, touching, and so on.
7. Help your child write a short story using only nonverbal communication to describe interaction.
8. Ask family members to role-play some events that relate to feeling states, especially those of the child. There could be a game in which the members try to guess what each is feeling based on body language.
9. Have family members write letters to each other expressing their feelings and how they express them nonverbally.

10. Watch movies and study how the actors express their feelings with their expressions, eyes, and body language.

TROUBLED EXPRESSWAYS

Mindsight is just one form of wordless communication. Your relationship with your child can also be affected, for better or worse, by
how you express yourself, including the tone and volume of your
voice. It's also true that the types of words you choose can impact
your relationship with your child. But 75 percent of most communication is accomplished nonverbally, which means that your words
are just one way to express your love and feelings to your child.
Let's look at nonverbal communication methods that may be even
more effective for building or restoring the bonds between you.

Mara, eight, and her mother, Joanna, had an unusual communication problem that brought them to my clinic. A beautiful child
with long black hair and golden brown eyes, Mara had been pushed
into child beauty pageants by her proud mother. By the time I met
this lovely child, she was a veteran of more than three hundred of
these contests. Her mother claimed that Mara was depressed
because she'd failed to win in her last ten competitions. Her daughter wanted to drop out and be a "regular girl," which Joanna considered unacceptable.

You might guess where my sympathies were in this case. I
strongly advocate that parents emphasize internal beauty over
external appearance. I could see that Joanna had set her daughter
up for failure, and for a life of low self-esteem, by putting so much
emphasis on competing for beauty crowns. I was surprised, however, when Joanna did not offer much resistance to my advice. I told
her that her daughter's depression and low self-esteem stemmed
from an unhealthy emphasis on external beauty. Joanna proved to

be very insightful and willing to accept my diagnosis. She welcomed my therapeutic suggestions too. Mara also seemed to be excited about a new approach. She had tired of the high-pressured existence, the continuous demands that she always look her best, and a life with no downtime.

I had high hopes that this mother and daughter would work together to repair their strained relationship. But then we hit an unexpected roadblock. When Joanna tried to communicate with her daughter outside of the peculiar jargon of children's pageants and that competitive environment, she adopted a vocabulary that only confounded the kid—and her therapist as well.

I once heard Joanna say this to her eight-year-old daughter, and I found it so odd I wrote it down:

"Mara, darling, you are much more than an android with the indistinguishable features of an endemic ill-bred hound. You have the essence of a soul to soar with angels within your heart."

Well, okay. There is something to be said for rising above street vernacular and slang. But you have to know your audience too. I didn't think there was any chance that the typical eight-year-old could grasp much of that. But it wasn't just the language used. Joanna spoke in the overwrought, dramatic tones of a junior high thespian. She had a vocal range that ran from an operatic bellow to a whispery baby talk. I had a talk about talk with Joanna. She agreed that there might be a more effective way to communicate with her little girl, especially after I played her a tape recording of her "Mommy Dearest" voice.

To her credit, Joanna toned it down. Mara responded immediately and eagerly. She was thrilled that she could have "girl talks" with her mother, and they quickly bonded into one of the most loving mother-daughter relationships I have ever witnessed. A simple adjustment in parental communication worked wonders in their case.

Quiz: Tuning In to Your Child

Your problems forming loving bonds with your child could be linked to miscommunication too. Take a few moments to administer this assessment. It can help determine if there is a need to consider some changes in how you communicate with each other. For each of the following statements, note whether each is true all the time (T), true most of the time (MT), true part of the time (PT), or never true (NT).

1. My child never seems to hear me when I give directions.

   T   MT   PT   NT

2. My child misinterprets what I say.

   T   MT   PT   NT

3. My child cannot tell whether I am serious or kidding around.

   T   MT   PT   NT

4. We never sing together.

   T   MT   PT   NT

5. I rarely can help my child relax.

   T   MT   PT   NT

6. My child and I do not understand each other.

   T   MT   PT   NT

7. I get angry or confused when we talk.

   T   MT   PT   NT

8. I do not understand my child's feelings.

   T   MT   PT   NT

9. My child's interest in me is limited to what I have to give.

   T   MT   PT   NT

10. Our conversations end in frustration.

    T   MT   PT   NT

11. In our home there is a lot of silence.

    T   MT   PT   NT

12. We just talk about everyday things.

    T   MT   PT   NT

13. I find my child's voice irritating.

    T   MT   PT   NT

14. I take pleasure in our conversations.

    T   MT   PT   NT

15. I yearn for better communication.

    T   MT   PT   NT

Assessing Your Answers

For each time you marked a T, score 5 points, and for each time you marked MT, score 3 points. For each time you marked PT, score 1 point. Add the scores together for a total in the range of 0–75 points. Compare your score to the following ranges and interpretations.

45–75   Your relationship bonds are fragile and could disintegrate in a crisis.

30–44   Improved communication could help your
          relationship thrive.
15–29   Communication training would be helpful.
0–14   Your communications appear to be within average
          ranges, but there is always room for improvement.

SUBTLE COMMUNICATION

How many times have you heard a parent say to a child: "I don't
like the tone of your voice"?

It works both ways. And parents don't give up any of their
authority when they tone it down to improve two-way communication with their children. Sounds trigger reactions in the body and
the brain all the way down to the cellular level. (And I'm not refer-
ring to your cell phone service.) We communicate our feelings and
emotions not just in the words we speak but in our tone and volume
as well. We also respond to tone and volume, and the auditory
vibrations these create within our bodies.

I've done a great deal of research on this topic with Dr. Mark
Rider in the Music Therapy Department of Southern Methodist
University. We've found that specific rhythmic sound patterns create
specific emotional responses. It will come as no surprise to rock
music fans that intensive drumming induces some sexual feelings,
for example. We also found that the march tempos that characterize
military marching music tend to induce feelings of self-confidence,
which explains why some of the armed forces use them for their soldiers. Perhaps most interesting, we found that a steady "heartbeat"
pattern on a drum induces a relaxed and secure mood in the listeners. We applied that finding by recording mother's heartbeats and
playing them over the sound system in a pediatric burn ward, where
babies suffer horrific pain during the healing process. When the tiny

burn victims listened to this heartbeat through earphones, we detected behavior that indicated they felt soothed and more relaxed.

Our study into the effects of sound on human behavior also found that adults reduce the symptoms of stress by singing or humming songs. The best results seemed to be from childhood lullabies or spirituals. Sadly, those adults who could not remember any songs had the most difficulty with chronic pain.

We also investigated other natural sounds to see if they induced relaxation and well-being. We discovered five types of sounds that appeared to have that general effect:

- Ocean waves coming to shore
- Rain on a tin roof or splashing on leaves
- A woman singing softly
- Wind in the trees
- Classical instrumental music

I just received this letter from a parent who reported a breakthrough based on musical stimulation. "After seeing the episode with Dr. Lawlis on Dr. Phil's show, I made a CD of all my favorite show tunes that had drum music in them. It is part of my daughter's morning routine now. It has made a difference. She had the hardest time waking up. I always told her that she just needed to warm up the brain cells. Now I announce that it is time to get up and turn on the music. You can hear her singing and clapping as she gets ready. I stay away until she has had about 20 minutes of music. The marching song from *Les Mis*, 'Do You Hear the People Sing,' is the most effective on her." I love this work.

VOCAL CORDS

In working to heal your relationship bonds with your child, remember that the human voice can have the same soothing and restorative hypnotic powers as a beautifully played musical instrument. You can bring your children closer with this instrument by using it skillfully. We verified this by studying the physiological response of children to a group of experienced storytellers. We hooked the children up to heart rate meters, muscle tension monitors, brain wave (EEG) machines, and blood vasodilation measures (measurements of the restriction of blood vessels that often correlate with stress) and monitored their responses during the storytelling sessions. We found that some qualities in the storytellers' voices most positively influenced the children. Low and slow tones, a restful breathing rhythm, consistency of volume and pitch, and a humorous or upbeat tone helped build bonds between storytellers and their listeners. Storytellers with deep voices and deliberate speech patterns drew the children into their presentations by setting an intimate mood. Our monitors found that the children relaxed and were more receptive to the storytellers when they used long, calm, slow breathing patterns rather than more excited quick breaths. Storytellers who used humor also kept the children enthralled, relaxed them, and made them more receptive and alert to the message.

BODY LANGUAGE AND BONDING

There are at least 700,000 body language signs used in human communication. Of these, 250,000 are facial expressions. We learn many facial expressions from those around us, but most are universal and appear to be hardwired into our brains.

In Table 2, I list some common body language signs and how they are generally interpreted by children. Most are facial expressions, because these seem to get the most response from children. Keep in mind that body language interpretations can vary widely from one person and one culture to the next.

TABLE 2

Common Body Language

Facial Gesture	Common Meaning
Blank face	Disinterested or confused attitude
Single raised eyebrow	Questioning motivation or truth
Lowered brow	Anger or judgment
Raised eyebrows	Excitement
Wide eyes	Fear
Wink	Approval
Sideways look	Contemplation or remembering
Shifty eyes	Suspicion
Glare	Focused attention
Flaring nostrils	Stimulation and excitement
Pinched nostrils	Arrogance
Nose wrinkle	Unwanted information
Sneer	Distrust
Set jaw	Determination
Smile (not showing teeth)	Approval and joy
Droopy mouth	Unhappiness
Pouting mouth	Sadness
Clenched teeth	Anger or determination
Toothy smile	Delight, welcome
Lip biting	Anxiety
Chewing	Relaxation
Scalp movement	Change in attitude

HAND AND ARM BODY LANGUAGE

Our hands and arms are also used in communication. As most Italians know, gesticulation is communication! Children and animals (especially dogs and horses) respond well to hand and arm signals. I had a dog named Max that read my hand signals so well we developed a "math wizard wonder dog" routine. I taught Max to keep barking when I spread my fingers apart. Then I would ask him to divide 16 by 4. He would bark until I signaled him to stop after the fourth bark. My math wizard dog wowed many friends and children. Amazingly, Max was every bit as good as me at fractions, square roots, and multiplication!

Children are known to respond to body language as well as—or even better than—to spoken words. In fact, historians tell us that body language, or sign language, has been highly developed in many cultures. To help you better communicate with your child, and to increase your awareness of what you say through gestures, I have listed some of the most universal hand signs and their meaning in Table 3.

BODY TALK

There are six common purposes for body language as a communication tool for building bonds with your child, and with other people in general.

1. *Redundancy.* Body language can be used to say the same thing being expressed verbally. If you are sad, you show a sad face and sloped shoulders. If you are happy, you show a smile and have an uplifting voice. These attributes give your message greater credibility to a child.

TABLE 3

General Hand Language and Meanings

Behavior	Meaning
Arm extended, open palm out	Stop or back up
Fist raised	Hostility and aggression
Arm extended, palm down	Slow down or be calm
Index finger extended	Focus on object or person, or follow directions
Index finger pointed to head	Mental functioning
Both palms extended upward	Support and welcome
Gestures of content	Attempts to visualize content
Finger wrapped around chin	Contemplation
Finger in mouth	Anxiety
Cold hands	Stress
Back of hand on forehead	Grief
Rapid movements	Excitement and joy

2. *Substitution.* Rather than saying something aloud, you can use your body language to convey the message. My father's face would tighten and grow stern when I did something wrong. He did not have to say a thing to express his feelings, especially if he used certain hand signals. It was also true that when he smiled, I basked in his approval. A parent's body language can leave a lasting impression.

3. *Complementation.* This form of body language enhances your spoken message, as when you make a sweeping gesture to describe something large, or an extended hand to order a halt. You can also create a sense of urgency by moving your body in a running motion. You can also use tone of voice, pitch, and rhythm to convey intensity of emotion. Parents often are very good at using body language to communicate

disfavor, but they are more reticent about showing positive body language. Smiles and hand gestures can be enormously helpful in conveying positive reinforcement.

4. *Emphasis.* We can use body language to accentuate and punctuate our verbal communication. My mother used the air as her blackboard. She would give an order such as "I want you to take out the garbage and study for an hour," and then she would point into the air as if her words were written there for further study. It can help reinforce the original message in the child's mind.

5. *Contradiction.* Too often, I've seen parents tell their children they love them even as they stand with their arms folded and their facial features locked in stern expressions. Your body language and your spoken words should not contradict each other, not if you want either to be believed. Remember that nonverbal messages can be the most powerful form of communication. If they contradict your spoken words, the child will likely respond to the body language. Even if you find your child's scrawling on the kitchen wall amusing, you can't smile while telling her not to do it—otherwise, the kid will never take you seriously.

6. *Regulation.* These are signs we use to control communication. My grandfather stood up when he wanted to talk, signaling that the rest of us should shut up. Others extend their arms with palms out to get the same response. Keep in mind that your body language has a major impact on how your child perceives your spoken message.

THE PLAN

It's natural to consider yourself a good communicator, just as most of us think we are good drivers. But both are more subtle skills than they appear. I've devised the following exercises to help you hone your ability to communicate with your child in subtle ways that will heal and strengthen your bonds.

Day 1

Record your voice while interacting with your child or other family members. This would be especially helpful if you are discussing a crisis or challenge. After at least thirty minutes has been recorded, and the crisis or interaction is over, listen to the recording in private. Consider how you would react to your voice if you were a child. Could the child understand your words? What emotional signals are you putting out? Is it possible that your meaning and intent are mangled by your tone, speech pattern, volume, or other methods of delivery? Repeat the experiment as you try to improve your communication skills to gauge whether you are coming across more clearly, and whether the child is responding to your efforts.

Day 2

Play a game with your child in which you say something—a sentence or two—in as many different ways as you can while always using the same words. This can be done using different tones of voice, emphasizing different words or phrases, and adjusting volume, facial expressions, breathing rhythms, speed, and body language, as well as other variables. The listener's challenge is to correctly identify the emotion being expressed. The winner is the one who can say it the most ways. For example, let's assume the statement is: "Take out the garbage." You can say it as a demand with a mean face—"TAKE OUT THE GARBAGE." Or you can say it with a singsong voice and a smile—"Take (da-da-da) out (da-da-da) the (da-da-da) garbage (da-daaaa)." Another way is to express it as a question—"Take out the garbage?"—with body language that says: *You talking to me?*

Day 3

Learn a song with your child so you can perform it together. It may be just a silly children's song or a jingle that makes your child laugh. Sing it together during the week, and then learn a new song each weekend. Sing together while driving, strolling, biking, or hiking. If you are musically inclined, learn the songs on whatever instruments you play, or drum the beat together.

Day 4

Train yourself to listen not only to what your child is saying but to her tone of voice and body language as well. For example, if your child discusses the school day in a very flat tone, respond to the tone: "You seem bored today," or "You seem to have something else on your mind besides school." Your child will feel closer to you because you are obviously tuning in. And as you get better at reading the emotions behind the words, you will be better able to communicate with your child in more stressful situations.

Day 5

Take turns acting as storyteller, describing a favorite event using gestures, descriptions, facial expressions, body language, and a range of tones, speeds, and volumes. You can describe a favorite adventure, meal, movie, sports experience, or family event. Make sure that you include the smells, sounds, sights, and emotions experienced. The storyteller should draw the listener in by asking if he too can see, hear, smell, and feel what is going on as you tell the story.

Day 6

Practice mimicking each other's breathing pattern. Make a game of this by being playful, but work your way toward a soothing, relaxed breathing pattern. You will find that this exercise draws you and your child together in powerful ways. I learned of that power while working with kids in a cancer ward. I trained parents to breathe in relaxing patterns to minimize stress during painful medical procedures such as spinal taps. I'd get parents to breathe deeply and at a relaxed pace, and often the child would mimic that pattern, which appeared to ease not only stress but pain as well.

The most beneficial breathing cycles are equal exhalations and inhalations, lasting about five seconds each phase. You can count to yourself as you breathe out to a count of five, and breathe in to the same count. It is harder than you think, especially when you are nervous or anxious. But if you do it successfully, with your child mimicking your pattern, deep bonding can occur.

Day 7

Go to a zoo with your child and take photographs of animals at play, grooming, nurturing, feeding, and even fighting. Then study photographs in books and magazines that depict humans in the same situations. Talk about similarities in expressions and postures. Then note how you and your child interact. Discuss the similarities or look for body language that might convey positive relationships. Tell your child to see if a family pet responds to body language, particularly "play" postures.

Day 8

Watch a movie with the sound muted. Afterward, discuss your interpretations of what the actors were saying and feeling. Note how your child interprets body language, and apply what you learn to your own nonverbal communications.

Day 9

While having a discussion with your child, try to mirror his body language with your own. For example, if he is slouching and crossing his legs, do the same. If he is talking to the ceiling in your conversation, talk to the ceiling as well. As you do this, try to understand how it feels to be in your child's position. Discussing this will help your child feel that you are trying to understand him better.

Day 10

Take turns giving feedback for each other's body language. Play out specific scenarios, such as when you come home from work or when your child comes home from school. Discuss specific gestures or movements and how they might be interpreted or misinterpreted. This can be fun, so take it lightly. This is a good way to be aware of what you do as well as how your child reacts. I bet that your child can tell you more about your body language than you can tell your child about hers.

Optional: Draw pictures of each other's faces, depicting a range of emotions. Talk about your interpretations and how they can differ. Test each other to see if you can really tell what the other person claims to be expressing. Again, have fun with this. Don't be afraid to get silly and enjoy the moment too.

Or take turns telling a funny or sad story using body language to emphasize or support the words. Make suggestions to each other for ways to add to the story with body language.

FINAL NOTES

The power of wordless communication should never be underestimated when you're working with children. They are finely tuned receivers for this sort of expression. When I'm working with troubled youngsters, I find that nonverbal forms of communication are often the most useful tools for breaking through to them. I urge parents to use these tools for building intimate, loving bonds.

We often do more harm than good with spoken words because they imply more than they deliver. We think we know what they mean, but many times we don't express ourselves clearly in words.

One day I was visiting a great-aunt and -uncle in West Texas. They were shelling beans, which they had often done together in their fifty years of marriage. As we discussed news of the day, my aunt asked a very ordinary question of her husband: "Do you want me to get you some of that coffee I made this morning?"

He nodded, and she walked into the kitchen.

While she was gone, my great-uncle smiled at me and said, "You know, she has been asking me about that coffee for most of our married life, but you watch; she will bring me out some tea. I believe she decided long ago that I don't really like coffee, so she brings me tea. I don't tell her any different. It might hurt her feelings."

Words don't mean as much as the emotions behind them. In this case, it was a deep and abiding love. We play on words and make rituals out of them. And sometimes we make our own meanings. In the end, it is not what you say, but what you do and feel that is most important.

6

The "Sour Brain" Phenomenon in Children

This is the fifth segment in the 90-day program. This chapter looks at physical and medical factors that can destroy or greatly inhibit your ability to form loving bonds with your child. If environmental factors or drug abuse are causing toxic reactions in your child's metabolism, you need to seek professional treatment. This chapter will help you make that determination. It should take five days for you to cover this segment. Again, if your child appears to have any of the conditions described, you should seek professional assistance immediately.

Loving relationships cannot be created, restored, or maintained if either you or your child lacks the ability to think clearly and coherently. The best guidance will do you no good. Both parties have to be clearheaded. Many times, I've had to delay or call off therapeutic treatments because we've realized we were dealing with a "sour brain." I coined that term for those minds that are crippled by chemical pollution of one sort or another.

Relationship building requires sensitivity toward others. It requires focused attention and concentrated effort. You cannot restore a relationship with a "sour-brained" child, just as you cannot reason with a drunk person. Neither can think straight. Neither has the ability to master new approaches to learning or to relationships. Parents who try to build or heal their bonds with sour-brained children are wasting their time, and may only be making things worse. I've seen it time after time, and I've included this chapter to alert parents.

Little Joe, eleven, was dragged into our clinic by his frustrated father, Joseph Sr. The boy had a vocabulary rarely heard outside of exorcisms and porn movies. His school offenses included groping girls and smoking. He came to me because his school wouldn't let him come back without a psychological examination. In our first meeting, Little Joe pretended to nap while his parents poured out frustrations and anger. They said he'd been a "good kid" until the age of ten, when he seemed to become possessed by demons. His grades dropped from A's to F's, and his friends disappeared. All he wanted to do was stay in his room and work with his model airplanes.

It didn't take a forensic specialist from *CSI Dallas* to recognize the clues to Little Joe's dark transformation, but I held my tongue while keeping an eye on the boy for several hours that morning. I didn't ask him to do anything but drink water and talk to me now and then. By noon, he was growing increasingly agitated. I took him to a nearby park, where he began to sweat and then grew lethargic. We returned to the office, and around 3:00 p.m., I performed a brain scan on him, with his parents' consent. We sent him home afterward, to his relief.

The next day, the results showed that Little Joe's little brain was not functioning well. It was being short-circuited by a lack of conversion or balanced activity. Little Joe was blotto, intoxicated, stoned. His model airplane hobby was a cover for an all too common practice among young boys, who inhale or "huff" glue to get a high. Chemicals in the glue cause impaired brain function, and the damage can be lasting unless the practice is stopped early on.

Fortunately, we got to Little Joe before he had glued his brain beyond repair. We cut off his access to the glue and put him in a detoxification program. This was followed by neurotherapy to restore brain functioning through nutrition and the development of new pathways in the mind. Within two months, the able-minded good boy was back, but it would take a year to fully restore his mental strength. Only then did we give him counseling that helped him recover his lost friends and heal his family relationships.

SOUR BRAIN SIGNS

Little Joe's case is not unique by any means, but we also see many sour brain cases that don't involve drug abuse. Increasingly, the decreased brain function is caused by environmental factors. The brain is highly sensitive to environmental exposure, both positively and negatively. Our brains respond well to the soothing effects of scented flowers, to views of evening sunsets and the smells of an ocean breeze. They also suffer adverse effects from poisonous fumes leaking from sewers, or harmful chemicals that flow to the brain from tainted foods.

The brain is the organizational center, the control room, for most functions of the body. It depends on the rest of the body to nurture and protect it. Our immune systems have multiple defenses, including white blood cells that serve as the front line of defense when external enemies enter the system. They use poison to kill organisms and swallow them, usually killing themselves in the process. Yet those poisons emitted by white blood cells can also kill good tissue, including that of the brain. Your child will not respond to even the best therapeutic programs if brain function is limited by toxins of some kind.

ARE YOUR FAMILY BONDS STRAINED BY TOXICITY?

We live amid a toxic stew of pollutants, so it is entirely possible that your difficulties with your child might stem from environmental poisons. I advise parents to eliminate that possibility before assuming that drug abuse or some other exterior influence is responsible.

I've seen hundreds of kids over the years whose relationships and overall development were hindered by undetected toxins.

Kayla came into the clinic as a hard-edged ten-year-old with a defiant attitude and out-of-control anger. Her adoptive mother, Alma, told us her problems had become significantly worse over the previous year. Kayla had been adopted at the age of one by Russian-American parents with a sixteen-year-old son and a fourteen-year-old daughter. Religious people, they raised Kayla with strong ethical guidelines, which had helped her stay on track most of the time despite serious challenges.

Kayla's birth mother was a cocaine addict who passed her addiction on to her infant. The adoptive parents dealt with this as best they could, despite little or no training. The child was very sensitive to noises and had many allergies to foods, which is typical of addicted children. When Kayla became upset, there was no consoling her. Her tears escalated rapidly into screams of outrage. As she grew older, she managed her anger better, doing well academically and socially. But then, just as Kayla entered the tumultuous prepubescent years, her ability to manage her anger and hostility declined.

By the time she came to us, she'd been diagnosed as suffering from attention deficit disorder, oppositional disorder, and bipolar disorder. As you may have gathered, I'm not inclined to simply accept the labels or diagnoses placed on my patients by others. We performed a brain scan to gather our own evidence. The results did not show patterns associated with bipolar or attention deficit disorders. But they did indicate that Kayla had a condition known as "foggy brain," which caused problems with integrating and processing information. It is often the result of toxins in the brain.

Further medical tests found that Kayla had some mild food allergies, which would not explain her antisocial behavior. There were other indications, however, that the child was suffering from metabolic problems. We followed the symptoms and concluded that

Kayla had a rather inelegantly named condition called "leaky gut syndrome." This is a gastrointestinal disorder in which the intestinal lining of the digestive tract becomes more permeable, or "leakier," than normal due to repeated irritation. The small intestine is designed to allow tiny particles of digested nutrients to pass through its wall and into the bloodstream. But when irritated, the intestinal wall can become more permeable and allow larger, less digested particles and toxins to pass through.

The body's natural defense system recognizes these particles as foreign "invaders" and attempts to contain them, creating high levels of inflammation and a host of related problems. The results can cause aggressive behavior, anxiety, confusion, illogical thinking, mood swings, nervousness, and poor memory—all of which can frustrate both the child and her parents, because they don't understand the underlying causes. Kayla's junk food habits aggravated the condition. She was a big fan of foods that are high in processed sugar and salts, including hot dogs and pickles. Because of her medical problem and her diet, Kayla was slowly starving her poor brain of essential amino acids, vitamins, and minerals.

While leaky gut syndrome can be remedied quickly, and a proper nutritional program is easy to implement, Kayla's system had suffered a lot of damage from inflammation and toxicity. It took four months for her body to recover to a point where she began to think more clearly and to have a more normal range of emotions. We helped her restore her relationships also with a nutrition and exercise program embraced by everyone in the family. Slowly, Kayla began to emerge from her brain fog into a very alert and happy girl. Her mother and father report that they grew closer to her than ever before, now that she was finally capable of returning their love and affection.

Kayla's life was transformed from the inside out. Her relationship problems could be traced to serious physical challenges that were beyond her ability to control. Parents should always consider that their child's behavioral problems might be at least partially due to physical problems. Don't be too quick to conclude that your child is consciously being difficult or acting out for subconscious reasons. I've found that the reasons for relationship problems between parents and children are as varied and complex as families themselves.

This symptoms checklist considers various problems that could be forms of toxicity and immune dysfunction due to environmental exposures. Please check off any symptoms that apply to your child or family member.

Toxicity Problems Checklist

_____ Avoids social interactions

_____ Highly emotional but refuses to discuss feelings

_____ Denies having a problem

_____ Skin rashes and poor dental health

_____ Mood swings and anxiety

_____ Feels dissatisfied with life

_____ Seeks immediate gratification and lacks foresight

_____ Poor emotional control

_____ Dishonest with self and others

_____ No recognition of limits

_____ A persistent runny nose, especially indoors

_____ Hypersensitive skin or rash

_____ Itchy or red eyes

_____ Sneezing

_____ Difficulty breathing deeply

_____ Rapid pulse

_____ Emotional irritability

_____ Red ears or cheeks

_____ Stomachaches, especially after eating

____ Gas and bloating
____ Constipation or diarrhea
____ Diminished ability to read with concentration
____ Diminished memory
____ Cravings, especially for soy or corn sugar (syrup)
____ Sleep problems
____ Difficulty organizing or prioritizing work
____ Increased aggressiveness
____ Decreased energy
____ Roller-coaster emotions

If you checked off more than three of these symptoms for your child, you may need to investigate your environment to determine if toxins are interfering with brain function. Do not overreact or rush to the judgment that your child is abusing drugs. It could be an environmental toxin present in the air, in the house, or in food.

POTENTIAL ENVIRONMENTAL TOXINS

There are between 50,000 and 100,000 synthetic chemicals in commercial production, and new synthetics are introduced at the average rate of three per day. We do not know how this chemical stew is impacting each individual, but the data strongly suggests that we are all vulnerable to neurological damage and even autoimmune reactions. Even something as innocuous seeming as a new house can contain paints or carpeting that give off invisible toxic gases. Many people develop sensitivities, and their immune systems are compromised by histamine buildup in the brain. New clothes and sheets can often trigger similar problems. Three-fourths of the homes lived in today still have lead-based paint or lead pipes, which also can be the source of toxins. The tables on the next page offer guidance based on studies of the impact from environmental toxins.

Behavioral Effects of Heavy Metal Exposure

Cadmium (common from manufacturing waste)	Difficulty in communication in relationships
Lead	Impulsive behavior and violence
Manganese	Compulsive behavior in relationships
Mercury	Poor vision, learning problems, and delayed social abilities

Behavioral Effects of Exposure to Solvents

Ethanol (alcohol)	Inappropriate language; eating and sleep disorders
Styrene	Hyperactivity and lack of inhibition

Behavioral Effects of Pesticide Exposure

Organochlorines/DDT	Diminished problem-solving skills
Dursban (diazinon)	Decreased ability to follow instructions

A PARENT'S NIGHTMARE: STREET DRUGS

If environmental factors are ruled out, you must consider the possibility that your child's antisocial behavior is related to drug abuse. Street drugs have infiltrated every socioeconomic level of society.

Most studies find that more than 50 percent of students have used some illegal substance by the twelfth grade, ranging from cigarettes to narcotics.

Even casual drug use can disrupt families and destroy loving relationships. Children are humans under construction, and the introduction of powerful drugs and chemicals disrupts natural processes. Drug abuse throws off the already complex interaction of hormones with psychological development. Toxic substances create chemical imbalances that can have dramatic and lasting impacts.

A major message that is never made clear to children and teens about drugs is that they are the most vulnerable for permanent damage. There is a period during early adolescence in which the brain begins to prune away much of the existing structure of neurons, like the pruning of a tree, in order to develop specializations. I describe this process like splitting off at the frontal lobe and disconnecting the areas of judgment and sense of consequences from the rest of the body. No one can explain why this happens, but it is a consistent pattern, in which reasoning and the ability to forecast consequences are almost lost for approximately three years.

This pattern has been studied, and most recently it spurred a move toward reducing the federal funding of programs addressing high-risk teen behavior, such as teenage pregnancy and drug use. The rationale for this policy is that the brains of teens are naturally lacking in judgment at this time, and thus education will yield little positive results. I would oppose these recommendations, for the reason that teenagers really need structure and guidance during this time most of all.

If these kids start taking drugs, the substances can have a permanent impact, hindering normal brain development by interfering with the pruning process. If new connections to vital centers are not made, long-term problems may result. It is like a young tree having its branches seared by a forest fire, leaving permanent scars and disfigurement. I've known adults whose judgment resembles that of teenagers because they used marijuana as adolescents. If you have doubts about the real danger of children using street drugs, I invite you to visit my clinic as an observer. You will quickly learn, as I have, that the young people in our nation are under continuous assault by predators offering them drugs.

OVERMEDICATION WITH PRESCRIBED DRUGS

I also have a problem with the abuse of prescription drugs used to medicate young people. I acknowledge, however, that this can be a very complicated and delicate issue. I do not oppose all medications at all times; some can be great tools to help a child get refocused and gain enough concentration to get things under control and on track. I have seen clinically depressed children and children suffering from attention deficit disorder make great strides with the help of medications. Often, psychotherapy and counseling can be made more effective through the careful use of prescribed medications.

However, parents can feel pressured to use medications even when there may be healthier alternatives and even more effective alternatives. Too often, children are diagnosed with attention deficit disorder after quick interviews with parents or teachers. Using a full diagnostic battery of brain scans and neuropsychological tests, we discovered a 67 percent error in these diagnoses. We have seen children as young as three years old who have been prescribed harsh medications for this condition.

Depression and bipolar diagnoses have grown exponentially in the last ten years, with similar poor diagnostic practices. The psychiatric literature has long said that no one under the age of twenty-five should be classified as manic-depressive or bipolar—there just is not enough history to make a case. As I understand today's literature, we now may be able to predict this disorder in teens by analyzing their depressive episodes.

Yet children five and six years old are regularly being m dicated for depression and bipolar disorder. Antidepression medication like Prozac, which is prescribed for youngsters, tends to heighten suicidal thinking in teens. This has been studied extensively in Great Britain. Few medications have been tested adequately in clinical trials for their effects on children. The drug companies merely cut the dosage from adult levels and assume a similar risk factor. In truth, there is no basis for these recommendations.

One of my biggest concerns is that children who have been given heavy medication don't know what it is like to feel "normal." As a result, they don't know themselves. These kids don't have a sense of what it is like to function without medications. They have been numbed out, and they are not in touch with their feelings. Yet these young people must go through the same maturation processes as other children to learn to deal with life's problems. Those who have been placed on medication without therapy are psychologically underdeveloped. A child who has been on medication since the age of five will still have a five-year-old's level of maturity at twelve. No wonder parents of such children have difficulty building loving bonds.

If the child is emotionally stunted, there may be little hurt but there is also little joy. It becomes very difficult to reinforce a child if he cannot feel positive emotions such as love. There is little joy even in food or touch for such children, and thus no psychological currency to work with for behavior modification and relationship building. The natural roles of parents and children and their interactions are essential for healthy physical and mental development. We don't fully understand what happens if those relationships are disrupted by drugs, either illicit or prescribed. When a child becomes dependent on stimulants, whether Ritalin or methamphetamines or nicotine, it throws off natural physical and social development.

Parents too often are uninformed about drugs and their impact on children. That ignorance is dangerous. Your relationship with

your child can be disrupted as much by the drugs in the family medicine cabinet as by those sold on dark street corners. Here are some
of the more common drugs that we've found to be responsible for
family relationship breakdowns.

Drug Category	Effects on Bonding Relationships
Cannabinoids— hashish, marijuana	High anxiety; poor memory; euphoria; interference with logic and relationship skills
Depressants— barbiturates, benzodiazepines (Ativan, Valium, Xanax, Librium), methaqualone (Quaalude)	Lowered inhibitions; impaired judgment; confusion; inappropriate reactions to others; lack of trust; lack of interest in making an effort in close relationships
Anesthetics— ketamine, PCP	Depression; "roller-coaster" mood changes; problems with grounding of relationships; often panic or aggressive behavior, causing fear in relationships
Hallucinogens— LSD, mescaline, psilocybin	Altered perception causes distraction and distorted views of relationships, creating unrealistic demands; often, relationships become viewed as unimportant
Opioids and morphine— codeine, heroin, morphine, opium, oxycodone	Confusion about reality; addiction; depression; difficulty communicating; relationships given low priority; imbalance of values; lack of self-control, creating paranoia
Stimulants— amphetamine, cocaine, MDMA, methamphetamine, methylpenidate (Ritalin), nicotine	Unhealthy feelings of exhilaration; excessive energy; reduced need for nurturance; restlessness; dissatisfaction with others' support; paranoia; impulsive behavior; violence in relationships; addiction

STEP-BY-STEP TO RESTORING A LOVING RELATIONSHIP
AFTER TOXIC EXPOSURE

The *first step* in restoring or initiating a relationship with a child under the influence of toxins—whether from drugs or environmental sources—is to recognize the problem and control it. Stop the exposure, whether it is environmental or self-inflicted. If there are lead pipes in the house, replace them. If your water supply is contaminated, go to another source. If your child is abusing alcohol, prescribed medications, or other substances, get rid of them. Do not hesitate to call in professionals, including the police, if necessary. Get the advice of experts and follow it. If they feel a rehab unit or detoxification is necessary, listen to them. Understand that there is not a quick fix. It may take six months to get rid of the toxicity, and that marks just the physical cleansing. Be prepared to confront the situation with your child if the toxicity is related to drug abuse. I suggest this action plan of intervention:

- Base your actions on the goal of developing and maintaining a love bond with your child. The primary concept is that your child needs to be healthy and make good choices in life. You need to convey concern and love. Make it a positive time for renewal of your child's goals and dreams. Review the goals and dreams as a start for discussing how to achieve them. Remember, these are your child's goals, not yours.

- An appropriate time for the confrontation must be selected. Besides ensuring such things as privacy, do not try to talk to a child under the drug influence. Your message will not get through.

- The action plan is to develop a problem-solving attitude. Explain to your child why you are talking about this issue. Be specific, unambiguous, and focused upon drugs—not the child—as the primary problem. Your messages need to be simple and concrete in order to be understood. Describe the particular behaviors that have worried you, i.e., damage, drunk driving, loss of memory of events while drinking.

- "Confrontation" does not equal attack. Drug abuse can take on a life of its own. It is important to convey that the confrontation is about a child's drinking or drugging behaviors and not an attack upon her as a person. A harsh confrontation will only alienate her. A failure to adequately confront the person, however, only promotes denial.

- The range of reactions depends on the child's level of denial. The earlier in the child's drug use an intervention and confrontation occurs, the less resistance and denial there will be, and the easier it will be for the person to change. Some may need time to digest any confrontations. Angry responses should be interpreted as signs of frustration and anxiety, not hostility. The child may also try to change the subject by pointing out that you abuse substances as well.

The *next step* is to cleanse the child's brain of the elements clouding her mind and impairing her relationship skills. You can't counsel someone under the influence of toxic drugs. You have to clear the pathways for logical thinking. Toxic substances and their effects are not easily erased. Your child may suffer cravings, physically and psychologically, even for environmental toxins. The cleansing process can be frustrating for parents because it often proceeds in fits and starts. There may be setbacks, as physical withdrawal triggers emotional reactions. What does not destroy your family can make it stronger. There are opportunities during these difficult periods to build trust and open lines of communication. I know of two families who decided to take a trip around the world in their sailboat for a year with their sons during their drug withdrawal. Another family moved to a ranch house in the desert while their daughter completed her detox program. There are enormous benefits to be derived if you and your child can cooperate with each other in challenging times.

Some natural substances help detoxify a person's body, and I have listed a few here. But please consult your physician before entering a strong program. Consider using some of the recommended substances below:

Table of Detoxification Substances

Milk thistle	Liver detoxification.
Calcium D-glucarate	Allows for increased net elimination of toxins and steroid hormones.
N-acetyl-L-cysteine (NAC)	Acceleration of urinary methylmercury excretion in animals; reduces liver damage.
Alpha-ketogluterate (AKG)	Detoxifies ammonia; synthesized from urea in the colon; often associated with Rett syndrome.
Methyl sulfonyl methane	Copper detoxification; reduces rages.
Taurine	Inhibition of catecholamine oxidation in the brain.
Methionine	A sulfur-bearing amino acid found in animal protein that assists in the removal of heavy metals.
Choline	A neurotransmitter as well as a metabolism enhancer at the cellular level in detoxification.
Selenium	Detox of heavy metals; promotes mental clarity and reduction of violence.

MUNCH 'N' MEND

These "munchie" snack foods have certain detoxification qualities and can replace potato chips and crackers during the process. Their effectiveness depends on individual factors, so what works for some might not be as effective for others. Most will help the cleansing process in some way.

- Flax seed
- Fennel seed
- Licorice root
- Aloe vera juice
- Grapefruit pectin
- Papaya fruit
- Peppermint
- Ginger tea
- Lemon water

Some ancient, traditional natural treatments can also aid the body in eliminating toxins through sweat glands, urine, and other natural processes. Native American healers used sweat lodges. Other cultures believe in the healing power of hot saunas, using sesame and juniper oils. Physical exercise enhances the body's natural immune system and helps cleanse it of harmful toxins. Professional masseuses also have treatments for healing and cleansing the body.

The *third step* is to begin the reconstruction process. You have to nurture both brain and body. As you become stronger, you can start making better choices for your life. You can gain insight and actually find solutions through new approaches for old problems. This should begin at the physical level.

NURTURING MEALS

My mother often interceded in family squabbles by announcing that we needed to stop arguing and eat. "Maybe everyone just needs a little something in their stomachs to make things work out," she would say.

I sometimes wondered about my mother's logic, but I never doubted her instincts. It always seemed to work just as she had predicted. We would eat and discuss as we digested. Maybe we were just more argumentative when we were hungry, but I think my mother also fed us foods that she knew had healing properties. She often fed us black-eyed peas and corn bread during these peacemaking meals. I've never found evidence that those two types of food have any special relationship-building ingredients, but I have done clinical studies on other foods that appear to help stimulate social interactions. I have served many of these foods in family therapy sessions, with good results.

It also is true that there can be a strong bonding effect when food is prepared and eaten for healing purposes. It is no coincidence that so many of our major holidays and social occasions are celebrated around meals. There is healing power just in the act of coming together to break bread. Some believe that this power can be enhanced by the attitude and imagery of the person who prepares the food. In some simple experiments, I discovered anecdotal evidence that there is a qualitative difference both in how food tastes and in its benefit for relationships, based on the emotional state of the cook. I had people with specific positive or negative attitudes prepare food and present the meals or munchies to others, who had no idea who had prepared it or what attitude they maintained. When we asked the eaters to rate the food and their reaction to it, the discrimination abilities were quite amazing. The food that was prepared by those with warm, loving attitudes tasted sweeter and more nutritious. The food prepared by those with a negative or cynical attitude gave the eaters stomach pain and nausea. This is fascinating, if not exactly scientific, stuff.

There are specific foods believed to help restore relationships, according to folklore and custom. In some cases, there is science to back up those beliefs. You may be surprised at the current science on some of these "basic" brain foods, but feel free to do your own testing. It couldn't hurt!

Water. I realize that this is not very sexy, although it can be found increasingly in pretty bottles at steep prices. Nevertheless, water serves as a major stimulator for neurotransmission in the brain. While there are obvious differences in water quality depending on the source, no one type of water appears to hold the edge on intelligence improvement. I'll leave it to your personal preferences when it comes to taste and purity.

Natural carbohydrates. The key word is *natural*. As noted earlier, too much unnatural sugar messes up the balance of your metabolism and drains your brain of energy. Natural carbohydrates include whole grains, fruits, and vegetables. They often serve as the energy sources for brain activity and have been related to positive relationships. Do not heat these before eating them. A fried tomato is not a tomato anymore; it has been chemically altered by the heat, and the extra sugar released does more harm than good.

Antioxidants. When the brain is insulted by things like alcohol and cigarette smoke, "free radicals" are released. Sometimes the immune system can get so confused, it begins to attack your good cells. This has been linked to autism and the toxicity of mercury and other heavy metals, with results described as the "unhappy brain." Free radicals keep the brain from using oxygen efficiently. Things go haywire in a process known as *oxidation*. You can see this reaction in other forms by observing the rust that forms on iron, or the spoiling of food.

Because the brain consumes more oxygen than any other organ in the body, it is especially vulnerable to oxidation. To protect your brain, you need to consume antioxidants. The chief vitamin antioxidants are C, E, B_6, and B_{12}. Other antioxidants include selenium, zinc, calcium, and magnesium.

Supplements have been shown to increase various functions, but real food is still the best way to get nutrients. Therefore, I recommend the following foods as major suppliers of antioxidants:

- Beets
- Red grapes
- Berries, especially blueberries and raspberries
- Red peppers
- Spinach
- Prunes
- Citrus fruits
- Sweet potatoes
- Carrots
- Tomatoes
- Onions
- Broccoli
- Asparagus
- Cabbage
- Brussels sprouts
- Beans
- Watermelon
- Wheat germ
- Nuts

Milk. "Nature's own soft drink" is rich in calcium, which offers many detoxifying benefits to the body. It can be useful in weight management and in treating cardiovascular problems. Other foods with high calcium content include calcium-fortified orange juice, tofu, low-fat yogurt, and turnip greens.

Turkey. This old favorite contains tyrosine and natural trypto-phane. These substances relieve anxiety and stress. They also tend to make you sleepy after Thanksgiving dinner—especially when combined with boring in-laws!

Beef. Meat doesn't get a lot of respect these days, but I give it good marks for mood enhancement, probably because of its high levels of iron (which reduces fatigue) and selenium.

Chocolate. In some cases, this candy is dandy. Dark chocolate has properties that enhance mood. It contains theobromine, a mental stimulant closely related to caffeine. Phenylethylamine (PEA), another ingredient of chocolate, is considered to be an aphrodisiac, which spawns a form of energy thought by Freud to be the source of all power.

Cinnamon. This is a great spice because it has no calories, even though it is a major taste stimulant. It is also a big aid for treating hypoglycemia (low blood sugar). Cinnamon contains a compound, methylhydroxy chaconne polymer (MHCP), that improves the body's management of blood sugar.

Honey. Bees deserve our respect. Honey is loaded with natural tryptophane, the natural precursor to serotonin, and a happiness transmitter.

Bananas. Bananas are a source for tryptophane and potassium, big players in stress and pain management.

THE PLAN

Day 1

Assess your environments and lifestyles and determine if you are exposed to toxic elements. These levels of toxicity may be the external sources of heavy metals and other chemicals that have been shown to injure the brain. Also, include your own toxic behaviors, such as substance abuse. Remember that sugar and grease are also toxic if taken in abundance. Take a good look and be truthful. You can change only what you acknowledge.

Days 2–3

If you can't find a good center to test whether you are holding a toxic substance in your body, then go to this exercise. Do a cleansing process for two days. Consistent with the oldest forms of medicine we know, perform some of the techniques discussed in this chapter. For example, you might do a cleansing diet using lemon water and take saunas for a day. You might take selenium and drink aloe vera juice for another day. Be restful and release as much toxicity as possible. If you have taken substances such as nicotine or alcohol, you might need seven days for a complete cleansing. Note how you feel afterward.

Days 4–5

This is the time to build your brain strength so you can receive love in the most powerful way. Take action to strengthen your system. I would heavily recommend exercise, especially rhythmic exercise, such as dancing, walking, and gentle yoga. This will strengthen the brain connections to the body and heart. Eat good nurturing meals with those who love you, and enjoy the power of vitality.

FINAL NOTES

Environmental contamination is a growing problem that will plague our world and our health for decades to come. We seem to stumble around, trying to fix one problem, while forever creating new threats. Cholera, for example, was found to be a direct result of diseased water. We controlled it by adding chemicals to our municipal water systems. However, scientists found that one of those chemicals, chlorine, could be carcinogenic, so nearly a third of the nation's water works switched to a substance called chloraine. All appeared to be well and good in major cities, until researchers discovered high levels of lead as a result of adding this substance. Chloraine appears to act with other agents to release lead particles from interior surfaces of plumbing.

Other problems have yet to be solved. The burning of petroleum products will always be problematic for our health. There are many concerns about electromagnetic waves and their impact on health. Toxins from chemicals in our homes, cars, and offices also threaten our well-being. We are just beginning to see the impact this has on large numbers of people with compromised immune systems.

Mother Earth is a wondrous place. Our bodies are miraculous creations. Yet, both are being subjected to environmental insults that neither is equipped to handle. We have used and abused our world, and now we are facing the consequences. Global warming is simply one of the most obvious impacts. Others may not be as apparent for many years, but I hope that this chapter has made you more attuned to environmental and other factors that may be affecting your ability to establish loving and lasting bonds with your children.

7

Managing Your Child's
Roller-Coaster Energy

This is the sixth segment in the 90-day program. In this chapter, you will be provided tools for managing your child's emotional energy, both positive and negative, in constructive rather than destructive ways. Too often parents make judgments or get defensive when dealing with their children's roller-coaster emotions, straining the bonds of love when they could and should be strengthening them. Children need to be taught how to control their autonomic systems. I will provide parents with methods and exercises for doing that in this segment, which will take ten days, including two weekends, to complete.

Parents with high-energy kids might fantasize about the Victorian ideal of children who are seen but not heard, but the reality is that most young people are not inclined to be docile, nor are they easily controlled. And that is probably the way it should be. Robotic children tend to grow up to be robotic adults, who have never learned to love or be loved. Energy, passion, and excitement are blessings that children embrace and adults praise. You don't want to pull the plug on your child's high energy, so let's look at ways to harness it instead.

Often, the parents who come to my clinic are those who have either gone too far, or not far enough, in their efforts to control their children. Overcontrolling parents aren't powerful—they are just overcontrolling. My goal is to help parents be nurturing people who give their children the opportunity to be creative and energetic while teaching them social skills, proper behaviors, and the difference between right and wrong.

Children can get rowdy. When I taught public school, I initially shared the fears of many teachers about being overwhelmed and losing control of my class. We had all seen movies like *The Blackboard Jungle* in which chaos rules the classroom. So I cracked the whip. Whenever student chatter reached a certain decibel level, I ordered the children to be silent—to be seen but not heard. But teachers have limited time with their young charges. It is one thing to ask for silence and strict obedience in a classroom setting. You cannot expect your child to be as controlled at home or in more relaxed environments.

Many parents make the mistake of cracking the whip, asserting constant control because they fear being overwhelmed. But when you do that, you risk trampling on your children's abilities to express themselves creatively—and you rob them of the opportunity to learn self-control. Parents who operate forever in the command-and-control mode are in danger of straining bonds of love and understanding that are essential for long-term relationships.

It is natural for children to be excitable. In groups, their energies can build to levels that adults have difficulty tolerating. But parents dealing with a child or several children at home need to allow them room for self-expression and for the expenditure of their pent-up energies in constructive ways. Tolerance is also a method for showing that you love your children, even when they aren't always in full control of their actions. It says you love them for who they are, in that moment. By allowing them to express themselves and to unleash their energies and excitement, you show that you are open to their individuality. This is the greatest of all gifts you can give your child.

Yet it is also the parent's responsibility to provide structure for children so that they can conform to society and its expectations.

Parents may find a child's imaginary playmates to be amusing, and they may even encourage them as an exercise in creativity. But when the child takes an imaginary playmate to school or to day care, she may face ridicule and social ostracism. In the same way, children who are allowed to "run wild" to vent their energies at home will likely rebel when teachers order them to take a seat and be quiet.

There has to be a balance, then, between tolerance and structure. When that balance is lacking, parents become frustrated, and children feel lost. Then they come to me or to other family therapists. Parents often tell me that their child has never been "normal," citing out-of-control crying, hostility, and rebellion at very young ages. Every day I listen to reports of children acting like "maniacs," impulsive, defiant, and unwilling to listen to reason. Parents often say that they've tried to be compassionate and understanding, but their children only take advantage of them until they have to threaten them or discipline them: "I want to be loving, but I have to play the drill sergeant to keep Johnnie under control."

In many cases, parents and children don't form loving bonds because of this constant battle over control. Very often this is the result of a developmental issue called lack of *autonomic balance*. Autonomic balance refers to the balance in arousal and restorative states in the body. The arousal state, called the sympathetic system, involves the physiological dimensions of higher blood pressure, quick breathing patterns, muscle tension, and heightened visual vigilance. Emotional factors include joy, fear, excitement, escape, and creativity.

Children are in an arousal state when they are excited and enthusiastic in their actions. There is a heightened expectation. You can see the muscles pumping, anticipating the next event. It is also evident when children are expressing fear and anxiety. Their voices are high and stretched, and they are hypersensitive to everything going on around them, seeming to draw energy from the air.

The restorative phases involve the parasympathetic system, which include the physiological dimensions of lower blood pressure and heart pace, slower breathing patterns, lower muscle tension, and soft eyes. The emotional correlates to these factors are relaxation, peaceful feelings, calm, and rest. For example, when a tantrum or laughing fit eases, a child enters a state of restoration.

The dynamics of the autonomic system allow for both passion and restoration. This is the juice of life. Yet it needs to be carefully controlled. I sensed that five-year-old C.C. and his adoptive parents were dealing with that issue during our first interview. His parents put it bluntly: "This was the worst mistake of our lives. We can't love this child, and apparently we can't love each other. Our marriage is going down the drain because of him. One of us is going to have to raise him, because we can't do it together," his mother said.

C.C.'s adoptive parents, Jennifer and Roger, were frustrated and frightened. They had adopted the Mexican boy after many years of trying, but failing, to have their own child. They'd found him through a child welfare agency and decided to "rescue" him. They were distraught at his apparent failure to return the love they had given to him, even minimally. He seemed to have no control over his behavior. Although they had been patient and encouraging, trying to make him feel safe and loved, he was out of control. They finally concluded that the boy just couldn't rise above his background.

His initials stood for Carlos Christian, but I had to dig for that information. He was a healthy-looking kid who rarely smiled. He shied from human contact and refused to look people in the face. C.C. showed affection only for his teddy bear, a bedraggled stuffed animal that had seen better days itself.

C.C. came to me with a diagnosis of autism, which had caused even greater despair for his parents. They had discussed the possibility of placing him in an institution, even though their original intention had been to give him a loving home for the rest of his childhood. They were good people who felt overwhelmed, and underqualified to give this child what he needed. After our initial discussions, I asked the parents to let me have some one-on-one playtime with C.C. I coaxed him into making eye contact with me by asking him to check to see if my eyes were working properly. He showed curiosity in agreeing to do that. I also got him to play a game in which we looked in a mirror and made faces for each other's entertainment. When he giggled, I knew there was hope. I playfully poked and prodded him to check out his physical condition, and he seemed to be a healthy boy, though his muscles were very tense. As I slowly got him to relax and let down his guard, C.C. became increasingly animated and excited. It was as if the child was emerging from a cocoon of caution and fear. As an experienced parent, I could tell that he was also growing tired, even as he became more active. It is typical for children of that age to respond to fatigue by cranking up their energy levels to maintain alertness. Soon, C.C. was literally banging his head against the walls, doing somersaults and acting like a hyper five-year-old. We'd established that he was capable of being a normal kid. Next, I had to teach him a few methods for controlling his energies.

I took the boy's hands and asked him to look me in the eyes and listen to me. I talked with him and asked him about his room at home and the items in it. As we spoke, I used soothing tones. I also breathed slowly and deeply so that he would pick up on those relaxed rhythms. I coached him to get comfortable and settle down so we could play some new games. He was reluctant to follow me at first because he was still wound up and feeling liberated with his parents out of the room. But gradually he quieted down, following my lead in his speech and breathing patterns.

We then played a biofeedback game. I hooked C.C.'s finger up to a skin thermometer and showed him methods for raising and lowering the temperature reading. Later, I gave him some computer games that allowed him to do the same thing, earning points by showing control. C.C. mastered the game, and in that session and others that followed, the boy began to emerge from his protective shell. As he became more self-confident and in greater control of his emotions—the goal of the biofeedback game—C.C. and his parents were able to form loving bonds and to build the foundation of a lasting relationship.

I also worked with his parents, teaching them how to relax C.C. through their facial expressions, their tone of voice, their touch, and their interactions with him. I encouraged them to play games and to sing with him as bonding exercises. I also advised them to display their feelings for each other more openly, so the boy witnessed loving behavior. As in many of my cases, the child's therapy included educating his parents about how to relate to him, rather than control him. Like many adopted children, C.C. feared being abandoned, and his adoptive parents needed to learn methods for assuaging those fears and for dealing with the emotions that accompanied them.

Interestingly, C.C.'s parents reported that the biggest improvements in their relationship with him came after small crises that drew them together. The boy lost his bear in the park one day. It shattered him when the beloved bear could not be found, but his mother spent the night holding him and nurturing him, and C.C. responded to her as he never had before. A few days later, C.C. fell and bruised his knee, and he ran to his mother immediately. She soothed him by singing to him and telling him a story, again drawing him closer to her. Over time, they became a team, and worked together with understanding and love. There were rough moments, as there are with most children, but both the boy and his mother learned confidence in their ability to get through such challenges and move on, thanks to their loving bonds. Their family therapist was touched too. It was especially rewarding to see the three of them settle into a loving family relationship and then to share the joy when Jennifer became pregnant. The boy responded well to this news, and he now has two little sisters who adore him.

CONTROL OF AUTONOMIC BALANCE

Children ramp up their energies when they get excited, a natural response from the sympathetic nervous system. But when children cannot "settle down" after a period of excitement, parents, teachers, and the little ones themselves can become frustrated. As a teacher, I had to deal with a class full of kids who were still "wired" from recess or lunch breaks. As a therapist, then, I devised methods for dealing with this through parasympathetic training.

One of the most intriguing facts I learned from my medical training is that the nerves for the parasympathetic system (the "brakes" that enable us to settle down our excited systems) run *to* the brain, not *from* the brain. This means that the best way to calm a child isn't to address her brain by commanding her to settle down. Instead, the child should be instructed to focus on her body by slowing breathing patterns, stretching, and relaxing the legs, arms, and hands. Relax the body first, and the mind will follow.

The Institute of HeartMath in Boulder Creek, California, is a nonprofit research center that examines the link between emotions and cognitive function, with the goal of helping people lead less stressful, more productive and fulfilled lives. The scientists there have done fascinating research with children and adults on parasympathetic training from the body up to the mind. Their methods include coordination of heart rhythms and breathing as a bridge to relaxation and calm. The HeartMath scientists have developed a device, called the EmWave, in which a tiny computer calculates the best breathing patterns to slow the heart rate to calming effect. Children love to use this small cell phone–sized device. Research has shown that those who use it do better in school and go to sleep faster. (A double bonus for parents!) Children benefit too because once they learn how to calm themselves they generally learn faster, get more done in less time, and grow more confident in themselves.

Assessing Autonomic Balance Control

For each of the items below, indicate how often you observe the behavior in a day: often (O), sometimes (S), rarely (R), or never (N).

1. My child gets anxious and cannot recover.

   O   S   R   N

2. My child clings to me when I try to leave.

   O   S   R   N

3. My child gets confused when asked to play quietly.

   O   S   R   N

4. My child becomes frustrated when asked to stop an intense activity.

   O   S   R   N

5. My child does not make eye contact with me.

   O   S   R   N

6. My child does not communicate with me.

   O   S   R   N

7. My child does not respond to my calming efforts.

   O   S   R   N

8. My child does not understand my calming efforts.

   O   S   R   N

9. My child is difficult for me to "read."

   O   S   R   N

10. My child is more difficult to control than other children.

    O   S   R   N

11. My child appears "lost" in a solitary world.

    O   S   R   N

12. My child makes me fearful of holding him when active.

    O   S   R   N

13. My child does not respond to my efforts to put him to sleep.

    O   S   R   N

14. My child does not respond well to my singing.

    O   S   R   N

15. My child does not respond to my efforts to draw him close to me.

    O   S   R   N

Scoring

If you marked O more than once, or S more than four times, it is likely that your child needs some help controlling his autonomic system. If you marked O more than five times, you need to read this chapter five times. Your child doesn't know how to balance out his autonomic system, and you don't know how to teach that skill. You are likely frustrated as a parent.

There are two critical elements for creating a sensitive environment for your child to flourish:

First, you must teach your children how to manage both high and low energy levels in a constructive manner. Unless they master self-control, children are ruled by their emotions and have difficulty fitting into social settings, school, day care, and, later, the work-place. They must be taught to judge whether their behavior is appropriate and to put the brakes on when it is not.

The second element is your own self-control. Parents teach mostly by example, whether they are aware of the process or not. What methods do you use to find joy and enthusiasm in your life? How do you change gears to relax and get off the treadmill? How do you balance your life and emotions? Your child studies your behavior constantly, looking for training and social cues. Your example will hopefully help your child find a comfortable level of behavior that allows for self-expression within socially acceptable boundaries. Children, even teenagers, often have to experiment to figure out what is acceptable and what isn't. This is often most noticeable when they try to be funny in the company of adults, using humor more appropriate for their peers or for the Comedy Channel than, say, Grandmother's bridge club group.

From a child's point of view, it's not always easy to figure out what is appropriate and what isn't. That is why they sometimes need help in reading external cues for social reinforcement. Too many times children misbehave simply because they are confused about the interpersonal "rules of the road." Their confusion often results in even more inappropriate behavior, turning simple social gaffes into disasters that Grandmother may spend years trying to forget. (If there is any adult who can't recall making at least one such childhood gaffe, I've yet to meet him or her.)

Children of a certain age, most notably those in their "terrible twos" and in their teen years, are known for their confusion and social ineptness because there is so much going on as their bodies and brains are undergoing transformations. Kids who are trying to find a balance in their energies need a lot of patient guidance and understanding. And they need to know the rules of behavior. Do not let a child in either group out of your sight without giving them guidelines. You can do this by laying down the law in talks with them. I'd suggest you get them calmed down and in a quiet place to do that. Repetition won't hurt. And, more important, you have to model the proper behavior for them every day, in every way. Sorry, no free passes for parents. (At least not for the first eighteen years or so.)

PARENTING STYLES

Children do not come with automatic transmissions that control the flow of emotions to their brains. Even so, many parents make the critical mistake of assuming their kids have both the brakes and the accelerator mastered. Actually, learning self-control is a lifelong process for most people; as we grow older we face new and different challenges, and the stakes get higher. It is extremely important, then, that you find the most effective methods for teaching your child to read situations and adapt behaviors accordingly.

Jerry, five, was delighted by the sound of his own voice. He loved to shout and sing, without considering that his outbursts might be disruptive for other members of the family. His parents felt that Jerry was just trying to get attention. They wanted him to learn when this was appropriate behavior, and when it was not. Let's look at four basic choices for dealing with Jerry's scenario, some of which are obviously better than others for the boy's long-term development.

1. His parents could ignore Jerry's outbursts until they become so disruptive that they cannot tune them out. Then they might tell him he is behaving badly, punish him, and order him to remain silent so that he does not offend those around him.

2. They could ask Jerry why he sings or speaks so loudly. Since Jerry doesn't know why, a battle of wills would likely follow. The

parents give Jerry an ultimatum, and he either shuts up or deals with the penalty for being disruptive.

3. Jerry's parents discipline him as soon as he makes an outburst, hoping to curtail the behavior.

4. (You've probably guessed that this is my particular favorite.) The parents follow a multiple-step plan. They first tell him to stop, even though they understand he loves to hear his own voice bouncing off the surrounding buildings. Next, they offer ways that he might calm himself, such as listening to soothing music or having a glass of milk. Then they offer him at least two options for channeling his energies constructively, such as going to his room and singing there, or playing on a swing set.

Parental response #1 is flawed because it denies the child's obvious need to release energy, and it shuts him down so fast and hard that he learns nothing about self-control, opening the door to possible avoidance and repressed feelings later.

Parental response #2 only increases the child's anxiety levels, while again failing to teach him anything about self-control and gauging his own behavior according to the social situation. Unfortunately, this is the most common parental response, which explains why we see so many children come in with high anxiety and lack of self-control.

Parental response #3 is potentially the most devastating to a child because it tends to trigger both fear and confusion. The child learns neither the joy of self-expression, nor the tools for socially acceptable self-control.

Parental response #4 is the most beneficial. Little Jerry is told "no" with clarity, which lets him know that he needs to get his behavior under control because he is pushing the boundaries of what is accepted. Even if he is immediately thwarted, he is offered options for emotional release. He is likely then to feel that his parents understand him and are willing to let him express himself as long as it is within the boundaries of appropriate, nondisruptive behavior.

It is the multiple-step method of discipline we endorse and teach at my clinic. It is important for parents to tell the child what the boundaries are and to alert him to the fact that he is pushing the boundaries or that he has gone too far beyond them. The key is to condemn or criticize the behavior, but not the child. The parent's next move is to offer reasonable alternatives for emotional or creative release. And finally, the parent should give positive reinforcement for the child's improved behavior.

TEACHING SELF-CORRECTION

Erica, sixteen, was brought to the clinic for fighting in school, defying authority, and waging war with her mother. She was short, slim, and tightly wound. She had been diagnosed at age eight with ADHD and was on medication most of the time. I found Erica to be an engaging kid. She was honest to a fault, prone to telling people what she thought for better or worse, and given to confessing every sin soon after commission. She kept her eyes on the floor when talking to me, which some adults interpret as disrespectful. Erica told me that she did this to indicate that she was remorseful for her behavior, not as a sign of disrespect.

Erica tended to think that adults were constantly judging her critically, or with pity. This perception put her on the defensive most of the time, so that she was anxious either that she might screw up or that she had already screwed up—which is precisely why she had such a hard time dealing with authority. This girl was harder on herself than anyone else could be, so their rules seemed like an unfair burden to her. (Nobody said kids weren't complicated.)

To help Erica learn to read adults more accurately, I pulled out the mirror—a tool that teens always find intriguing. I asked her to study her own expressions in the mirror and to give me her interpretations of what she appeared to be thinking based on them. She had difficulty either reading or interpreting her own feelings because she'd always been so focused on what others might be thinking of her. Poor Erica was so busy *reacting,* she had difficulty *feeling.* I told her that her homework for the next six weeks was to identify her feelings throughout each day and to write them down, while also noting the expressions she wore for each of them.

Once she'd done her homework and undergone therapy, the change in Erica's interpersonal behavior was astonishing even to me. She was instructed to identify her feelings instead of reacting to what people were telling her and trying to validate their feelings. When she learned that she could choose how to feel, no matter what others might say or do, it was a revelation for her. It may even have changed her life for the better.

In a very brief time, Erica was transformed from the typical problem child to a very thoughtful and well-behaved young lady. She learned that once she controlled her emotional responses, her teachers and her mother would give her more room to make her own decisions. They treated her with more respect because she had earned it.

Erica's successful transformation was the result of two decisions. She decided to monitor her emotions and to consciously choose constructive, rather than defensive, responses. Not all teenagers have her intelligence, nor do they have her desire to change for the better. But I never count anyone out. We are never too old to change our behavior, once we are given methods and encouragement to do it.

STRATEGIES FOR RESPECT

Like cars, we are all equipped with accelerators (the sympathetic system) and brakes (the parasympathetic system). Our gas and brake pedals govern our physical and emotional responses. Children need to learn how to operate both the accelerator and the brakes to control their energies so that they behave appropriately and become good citizens. Biofeedback therapy and body-mind strategy are two methods for mastering human driver's ed, but both should be administered by a trained and licensed professional. The following exercises can be administered by a parent to at least get the training started.

SYMPATHETIC TRAINING

The goal of these sympathetic training exercises is to encourage self-discovery and to heighten your child's awareness of emotions and sensations. While this comes naturally for most of us, some are slower to develop these essential skills. Often, children's behavior is taken for willful disobedience when in truth, they are simply lacking some basic skills. This is often true of children who are forced to take on adult responsibilities at a very young age. They are never given the time or opportunity to simply savor experiences and to monitor their emotional and physical reactions. These exercises are designed to provide that opportunity.

1. Play in the mud.
2. Walk in bare feet.
3. Paint with finger paints.
4. Tickle each other.
5. Write three-line poetry.

6. Tell jokes.
7. Play games like hide-and-seek.
8. Explore the sensation of being touched with love or having a massage.
9. Rock in a chair.
10. Sing.
11. Dance.
12. Perform in a play.
13. Cuddle.
14. Explore the body and how it works.
15. Walk on the beach.
16. Play catch.
17. Listen to the sounds of the day (animals, birds, etc.).
18. Play with animals.
19. Talk to a friend.
20. Discover a new place or share a secret.

PARASYMPATHETIC TRAINING

Parasympathetic training teaches the child how to put the brakes on energies and excitement according to the social setting and situation. It's one thing to scream out while watching a football game in the stadium; it's another to shout out while sneaking a look at a game in the office. The natural impulse is to go with the flow of the energy but social skills require that we put the brakes on in many cases.

While the high-energy child may balk at the thought of "putting on the brakes," as she masters these exercises, she often takes a great deal of pride in her newly learned self-control.

Encourage your children to:
1. Listen to relaxation training tapes, CDs, and other devices.
2. Discuss alternative responses to challenging scenarios.

3. Talk about their "destiny" based on talents and interests.

4. Learn effective breath control as a calming method.

5. Learn biofeedback methods to control stress.

6. Find ways to sleep well.

7. Discover acceptable ways to express their internal feelings.

8. Find emotional release in constructive ways.

9. Share feelings with another person.

10. Become comfortable with others.

11. Learn at their own pace.

12. Meditate or pray.

13. Dance to various types of music.

14. Play an instrument.

15. Do calming exercises (listening to music, counting breaths, etc.).

Learning how to love or be loved begins with the earliest years of development. It is possible for your child—and for you too—to overcome challenges and to build loving, lasting bonds by channeling your child's energies in beneficial ways. Your child needs your guidance to do that. Once your child learns to monitor inner emotions and to read those of others, the next step is to understand that while none of us can control what happens to us we can control how we respond. I encourage you to reach out to your child. It may take a lot of work and patience but it will be well worth it over the long term.

THE PLAN

Days 1–5

Select sympathetic training exercises, such as those found on page 152, and participate in at least one per day with your child. It is perfectly appropriate to include multiple individuals, such as friends and family. Make a note on how both of you experience each one and use each as a tool for inducing enthusiasm and expressions of love during the day or after.

Days 6–10

Select parasympathetic training exercises, such as those found on page 153, and participate in at least one per day with your child. It is perfectly appropriate to include multiple individuals, such as friends and family. Make a note on how both of you experience each one and use each as a tool for reducing destructive behavior due to overenthusiastic emotions during the day or after.

FINAL THOUGHTS

This chapter deals with perhaps the most common issue parents face: how to balance a child's need to express feelings with her parents' desire for her to stay within social boundaries. It takes great skill and judgment to maintain this balance. I've provided a number of tools and methods for doing that. It is also helpful for parents to take a step back and put things in perspective. Teenagers are not fully formed. Some day, your child will be an adult. Think of your child one day dealing with the same issues with a teenage offspring. Always keep in mind that you are not only a parent, you are a teacher, a mentor, and a role model for your adult-in-progress. You are forging bonds that will last for generations to come.

8

Feeling Leads to Healing

This is the seventh segment in the 90-day program. This segment serves as the keystone. To build loving bonds with your child, you need to understand each other's feelings, how they affect your actions, and how to best respond to each other. Because this segment requires significant practice and awareness, you will need ten days to complete it.

Our most basic human need is to be understood and accepted. If you want to have a deep and caring relationship with your child, you must learn to read, understand, and respond to your child's feelings by developing empathy. This ability to sense the feelings of others—to "read" their emotions and their motivations—is a very important skill, whether you are a parent, a priest, a car salesman, or a therapist.

When a client walks into my office, I have about fifteen seconds to make a "read" that determines how I approach the individual. For all of my education and experience, I depend more on my empathic skills, honed over many years and hundreds of patients, than any other tool. To be understood and accepted is a blessing and an antidote to loneliness. For young people, it is critical to their healthy development and to their ability to form lasting relationships. Native Americans considered empathy a spiritual gift, "to walk in another's moccasins for a day." A parent who strives to understand the emotions behind the child's words and actions rather than focus on what is said or done will likely build loving bonds for a lifetime. That doesn't mean you ignore disrespectful words or dangerous actions. It does mean that you first seek to understand rather than to condemn or to punish.

Parent-child relationships that lack empathy can deteriorate rapidly. I've seen it happen many times. Not long ago, I observed this exchange between Kate, twelve, and her mother, Hilary, just as they started to discuss the daughter's desire to have a late curfew.

HILARY: "Kate has always been such a bright, sweet girl, but now she wants to stay out all night. I don't see why she wants to do this so badly. She could have some girls over to spend the night."

KATE: "But Mom, you don't understand. I don't want to stay out all night, but I do want to be like my friends."

HILARY: "And what do I not understand, Little Miss Big Britches? I am your mother, I know you better than you know yourself! Until you're eighteen, you'll follow my rules. I won't allow you to run around all night and look like a tramp. All you want to do is act like a fool and embarrass me."

KATE: "So you don't trust me, then, and you think you know me? Well, I'll show you how much you know. You're nothing but a shallow freak who hates me! And I hate you!"

This mother and daughter were doing a lot of talking, but there was virtually no communication, no attempt to understand each other, and no empathy. Their conversation was all about lashing out at each other, returning blow for blow, hurt for hurt.

Too often, parents and children make assumptions about each other because of their familiarity, and it never occurs to them that those assumptions may have been wrong from the start, or rendered invalid by change. To render judgments based on false assumptions is to condemn a relationship to death. Nothing can come of it but more pain.

In labeling her daughter "a tramp," Hilary only adds to the girl's bitterness, hurt, and shame. It drives them further apart at a critical time when they need to be pulling together. After that conversation occurred, I talked with Kate and Hilary about trying to understand each other's motives and feelings rather than attacking each other. They got it, but only at the most basic level. As this later conversation reveals, Hilary tried to relate to Kate's feelings, but she didn't quite get it, triggering more conflict instead of empathic understanding.

KATE: "I want to go out Friday night to a football game where all my friends will be. It would embarrass me if I have to come home at ten."

HILARY: "You know, when I was your age I remember wanting to go out with my friends to a party, only it was a carnival instead of a football game. I begged and begged my parents, but they wouldn't budge. Until one day I caught my father by himself and I got him to let me. Well, it was a disaster. I got lost from my friends and finally had to call my parents to come get me. I was so disappointed."

KATE: "So you see why I really want to go."

HILARY: "I see you want to go because of your friends, and I already know you'll be disappointed. I was always disappointed, so I think you should be very careful. I know you will be disappointed."

KATE: "But I'm not going to the carnival, I am going to the football game. My friends are playing. This is a big deal!"

HILARY: "So go, but be back by ten sharp or I'll go looking for you. I just want you not to be disappointed. And don't go to your father."

KATE: "You really just want to be sure I will be disappointed, don't you, Mom?"

There is still no true communication in that exchange. They talk to each other, but they each focus on their own feelings without seeking understanding of the other's. They are two ships passing in the night, blasting warning sirens at each other. There is no connection. Instead of working together toward a mutually acceptable resolution, they resort to manipulation and lashing out—which is what happens when communications break down.

Now let's consider an interaction in which greater empathic skills are practiced. This is a conversation between Kate and her mother at the last therapy session. Both had worked hard to learn empathy. There were still issues between them that they needed to work on, but by this point, they were no longer engaged in constant warfare. They were on the healing track, building loving bonds.

KATE: "Mom, there's a party after the game tonight, and I would like to go and stay late. I know what you will say and how you feel, but p-l-e-a-s-e give me a chance."

HILARY: "I can see how you must be about to throw in the towel in asking me again, but I'm not sure you really know how I feel. I worry about you, and I guess I think that you might get hurt. I don't like to be the policeman, and it always ends up with me worrying."

KATE: "I guess I knew that you had some reason, but I need to grow up someday. It sounds to me like you're really afraid I will do something stupid, or someone else will, and you will feel guilty. Is that the way you feel about me?"

HILARY: "I do worry about me and you. I worry about my being a responsible mom, and I worry about something happening to you that I have no control over. When you are not here, my mind goes through a dozen horrible scenarios."

KATE: "So what it sounds like is that you're holding on to me for your needs instead of mine. Is that fair? I want you to come to trust me one day. I want to have you trust that I can be okay by myself. Otherwise, I will always be a little girl to you."

HILARY: "You're right; I need to trust you more. What I hear from you is that you want my trust. So we have these two needs, yours to be trusted and mine to be protective. You seem to be frustrated that our needs are competing with each other. I understand that too, but I wish you didn't feel you had to get mad to get your way."

KATE: "I guess I get mad because I don't think you hear me as an adult or almost an adult. I guess that puts us at odds, doesn't it?"

HILARY: "Let's problem-solve. If I understand your side, you want to grow up and be with your friends later, but the bottom line is to gain self-confidence. You get mad because you're frustrated and don't know how to get your way. You want to be trusted more. Right? And I feel I have to be in control, maybe too much. So I resist your efforts to be treated more like a grown-up as a result of my need to be in control. Right?"

KATE: "I guess that's right."

HILARY: "The next step would be to find a way for both of us to win. How can I support your desire to be treated like a more mature person while still allowing me to feel in control of your safety?"

This dialogue went on for six months. Kate and Hilary eventually worked out a method for reaching mutually acceptable compromises. They set up a format to present their feelings and needs and then worked together. Kate got to stay out on school nights for special occasions, and Hilary maintained a sense of safety and control. In the process, they came to enjoy each other's company so much that often they did things together that they otherwise might have done without each other.

This is a more direct and empathic approach to the conflict. Kate and Hilary worked harder to understand each other's feelings and motives without attacking them. Once empathy becomes the guiding principle, both sides can seek solutions instead of focusing on problems. They work together based on shared understanding instead of fighting over their differences.

Another interesting aspect of empathic communication is that when someone feels they are understood, they are more inclined to reveal their feelings. That is why therapists work at being empathic, because it reduces the inhibitions of their patients. This case involved a teenager who had verbal skills, but children of all ages, even those who cannot express themselves in words, can be and need to be understood. Adults should be empathic to them too, because it is a proven way to build stronger, loving bonds.

Quiz: Empathy Assessment

Is your relationship in need of more empathic communication? Are you running into the same set of resistances and frustrations repeatedly? Is your communication working for you? Here is a brief assessment to test your communication style, especially your level of empathic responses.

For each description, mark how consistent the portrayal of your communication style and results are with your child (or any person), by indicating always (A), often (O), infrequently (I), or never (N).

1. I am mystified about the behaviors and attitudes of my child.

A   O   I   N

2. I feel that people don't understand me.

   A   O   I   N

3. I feel that my conversations with my child always come to a stalemate or confrontation.

   A   O   I   N

4. I try to focus on the behavior and change it.

   A   O   I   N

5. My child seems uncomfortable talking about feelings.

   A   O   I   N

6. I wish my child and I could talk more easily.

   A   O   I   N

7. I wish I understood my child better.

   A   O   I   N

8. I am afraid of what my child thinks of me.

   A   O   I   N

9. Our disagreements escalate into areas I don't even care about.

   A   O   I   N

10. I don't know how to talk to my child.

    A   O   I   N

11. We do not understand each other's point of view.

    A   O   I   N

12. When my child and I talk, it is only for a few minutes.

    A   O   I   N

Scoring
Count 2 for each A, 1 for each O, count ½ for each I. Add up the 12 scores for a sum that will range from 0 to 24, and compare it to the ranges below.

16–24	You need communication skills, especially the skill of empathy.
9–15	You have good connections with your child, but you could be more sensitive of feelings.
0–8	You have good communication skills with your child.

DEFINING EMPATHY

Most people feel they are empathic to some degree. Of course, software engineers worry less about it than social workers, because it plays less of a role in their work lives. But we all need empathy in our personal lives if we are to have lasting, loving relationships. Parents need it in particular so that they can tune in to the feelings and the needs of their children. There are varying levels of empathy, and it is possible to increase your own with training and practice. In Kate's case, three levels of empathy were demonstrated. When I train psychotherapy students, it always strikes me that there are many different ways to express empathy to others. For some, all it takes is a nod or a look of understanding to communicate that you comprehend what the other person is feeling. For others, it takes clear verbal communication or physical touch.

Empathy is an interpersonal skill—a gift or talent as much as athletic prowess or musical ability—that tunes in to the feelings of others while also communicating understanding and insights. Your most empathic friends are those you go to when you need to talk about something that is troubling you or that excites you. Empathic people have the shoulders we cry on, the strength that we lean on, and the hearts that share our joy.

People described as "cold" often send out that vibe because they lack empathy. They tend to suppress their own emotions, for whatever reason, so they are not attuned to the feelings of others. I've seen physicians who appear to lack empathy because they've developed a "thick skin" after years of dealing with pain, suffering, and death. But empathy can be a valuable tool for physicians seeking to better understand their patients.

The lack of empathy and an inability to express emotions can be signs of anger management problems and other antisocial behaviors. Studies of men arrested for domestic violence find that they have limited abilities to express their feelings of anger in nonviolent and socially acceptable ways. As a result, instead of venting their emotions safely, they lash out physically. The therapeutic approach to anger management is to attempt to give the patients greater empathic skills and a wider range of ways to express their feelings in constructive, or at least nondestructive or not hurtful, ways.

Anger is not the only emotion lurking within us, of course. There are at least three thousand words that depict emotional states. Here are a few that appear to be more common:

Fear	Anger	Happiness
Sadness	Satisfaction	Grief
Security	Annoyance	Rage
Confusion	Depression	Anxiety
Contentment	Gloom	Sorrow

Misery	Pain	Seclusion
Joy	Bliss	Elation
Melancholy	Confidence	Ecstasy

GETTING A READ

Professional poker players are often highly skilled at picking up "tells," or nonverbal cues that their competitors at the table display in certain states of mind. To be sensitive to the feelings of others, you must learn to pick up on not just what is said but also subtle cues including tone of voice, body language, and facial expressions. Downcast eyes, slowed speech, and slumped shoulders depict depression or grief, just as the furrowed brow, lip biting, and upheld palms express concern. Think about the emotional cues your child displays, and what they mean. For each emotional state listed below, write down the visual, auditory, and bodily signs that are associated with them. If you cannot think of any, do some exploration with your child and add new dimensions. Also, add the cues you display and the feelings they are associated with.

Emotional State	Child's Cues	Your Cues
Fear		
Anger		
Happiness		
Satisfaction		
Grief		
Confusion		
Depression		

Emotional State	Child's Cues	Your Cues
Anxiety		
Contentment		
Pain		
Seclusion		
Joy		
Bliss		
Security		
Confidence		

COMMUNICATING EMOTIONS

If there is some question as to how your child is feeling, it is okay to ask. It might help to provide a list of possible emotions if you get the usual "I don't know" response. Kids give that answer routinely, but it is also likely that your child does not know how to express feelings. His emotions might be layered and complex. Many individuals, especially children, confuse hurt feelings with depression and anxiety. Anger and frustration are similarly confused. Even joy and fear can cause similar reactions, such as trembling or nervous laughter.

Psychotherapists spend much of their time simply clarifying the emotions of their patients in order to understand their behavior. Confused emotions lead to confused behavior, just as very clear emotions lead to clear action. If someone hits you for no reason, you don't have much problem figuring out a response. But if you are struck because you made a nasty comment about the person's family two weeks ago, determining your response can be a bit more complicated. Clarifying the emotions that lie behind your child's behaviors is essential to clear communication and to the long-term health of your relationship. Once you learn to recognize your child's emotional states, you can respond to them in ways that draw you closer.

THE INTERACTIVE INGREDIENT OF EMPATHY

A parent's real challenge in empathic communication with a child is learning to convey that you understand and are willing to help. Sometimes a smiling nod or simply the words "I understand" may be all you need. But it might take more than that. You may have to tell your child specifically that you understand the exact emotions in play, so your attempts to help are well received. One way to do this effectively is with the "mirror reflection" approach. Suppose your child says, "I am so mad I could hit you in the nose." A mirror response would be, "You really sound mad at me, probably because you are hurt and want to hurt me back," or "You sound like you are angry and frustrated."

The mirror reflection approach communicates to your child that you are listening, that you understand, and that you are responding to his feelings, not his words. It sounds simple. But there is an incredible amount of healing power in that message to your child.

Consider some of the other examples of mirror responses below.

Statement	Mirror Response
"I am sad and tired."	"You seem pretty tired and sad."
"I really hate myself."	"You must really be down on yourself."
"I want to just run away."	"You sound like you want to just run away."

Statement	Mirror Response
"I want to burn the house down."	"It seems like you want to destroy the house and everything in it."
"You are mean."	"You feel like I am not being nice."
"You are being unfair."	"It sounds like you think you are being treated unfairly."
"You are a liar."	"You feel like I have told you a lie."

Again, while these responses seem fairly simple and straightforward, research has shown that they will serve you well. Your child will be far more likely to trust you and communicate openly with you when you respond in this way. I tell my student therapists that if they ever get to a point when they don't know what to say, the best response is a mirror response. It is a method for opening up dialogue and discouraging conflict.

The next stage for encouraging deeper communication with your child is an empathic response that reflects the trigger to your child's emotions. It helps to couch these responses as guesses or questions rather than as stated facts, so that the child doesn't get the sense that you're making judgments. Suppose your child said, "I hate you right now!" Your deeper empathy response might be, "You are probably mad at me, and I think that you may be frustrated with me because I may have embarrassed you in front of your friends. Is that right?"

These empathic responses may require some guesswork if you don't know exactly what is going on, but it won't hurt to be wrong as long as you are careful in how you couch your response. Your real goal is simply to keep the communication going and move deeper toward the source of your child's feelings. Even if you are wrong in your initial assumptions, your child will appreciate that you care enough to try to understand.

BREAKING THROUGH

At this point, you may be thinking, "This will never work on my kid." Maybe not. But I've seen these methods crack some very tough cases, often with remarkable speed. Nora was one such case. The twelve-year-old girl had been in therapy for depression for two years when another psychologist referred her to me. She was obviously unhappy, withdrawn, and never completed any assignments in school. She had refused to talk to the other psychologist, her parents, her teachers, or anyone else, according to her records.

My initial efforts to draw her out met with the same silence that she had rained upon all others.

"Nora, it looks like you and I are supposed to talk about some things. Can you tell me how you feel today?"

(Silence.)

"Nora, I am going to assume that you don't communicate with me because you are angry. That is what a lot of angry kids do, they just don't talk. And from your expression, I would have to guess that you are not a happy girl."

I then showed Nora her reflection in a mirror. (Always a good move with girls her age.)

Nora began to show some interest, at least in her reflection.

"Do I look like I'm mad?" she said, studying her image.

I relaxed my breathing so that my voice remained calm and controlled, which had a calming effect on my patient as well.

"I would say that was my impression, Nora. But you seem surprised at that. Are you?"

"I don't guess so. Yeah, I'm tired of people poking at me, and I don't like it."

I was on a roll!

"It sounds like people have really put you through the wringer. Tell me how this started."

"It all started back before I can remember, when my mother was making me sing. She thought I was so cute, but I was embarrassed."

"So if I am hearing you right, this was your way of avoiding embarrassment. You stayed quiet, and you kept silent even when they took you to therapy. Sounds to me like you got to them. They gave up trying to crack your shell."

Nora chuckled at the idea that she was a tough nut to crack. "Yeah, I'm a tough nut all right."

"But if I had to make an educated guess, I would bet that your silence has something to do with anger about your mother pushing you to perform for her. Is that right?"

Nora gave me a thoughtful look, paused, and then all but handed me the key to her therapy with this profound statement: "That battle has been going on since I was a baby."

The breakthrough had occurred. Simply by practicing empathic listening and mirror responses, I was able to win the trust of this troubled young woman who had refused to talk to everyone else. After that, we entered into a series of long and intimate conversations. By midway through the second session, I could hardly get in a word; heartfelt thoughts and concerns poured out of Nora. The dam had broken. Once I taught Nora's mother how to communicate empathetically with her, my work was all but done. The last I heard, Nora was even singing again, but now it was for her own joy, not at her mother's command.

TRY RELATING, NOT DICTATING

The key to practicing empathy is to remember that the goal is not to change your child's mind, or even to resolve a problem. Your goal is to show your child that you are trying to understand the feelings behind her actions. There is great healing in that. The primary need of your child is to have those feelings recognized. It is as simple, and as powerful, as that. Once you have convinced your child that you recognize those feelings, then and only then will the lines of communication begin to open.

To get communication flowing, you should resist all parental impulses to try and "fix" the situation. Instead, try sharing your own feelings in a way that relates to those your child is experiencing. This approach requires some finesse, because you don't want to assume your situation is the same as your child's. It shouldn't become a contest over who hurts more, or who is more confused, or angrier. Instead, be honest in telling your child how you feel and that you've been in similar situations. Lay the groundwork for the healing that will come.

Share your feelings directly or within the context of your experience. The operational term is "feelings." Not advice! Resist the temptation to make judgments or suggestions. Don't rush the process. If your child screams that she is angry with you, you might reply by revealing, "I used to get mad at my mother too. I would get so mad when she was unfair. Is that the way you feel toward me?"

Another approach is to tell a (brief) story in which you experienced similar feelings. The beneficial part of this strategy is that you can add an ending with a positive spin: "When I was about your age, I thought my mother was the most powerful person in the world because I counted on her to do things right. But she disappointed me when I thought she was wrong. I would get so mad at her that I wanted to strike out. Sometimes she was wrong, and she wouldn't admit it. I would stomp around for a couple days. But then I decided that moms make mistakes too. And it really didn't make me feel better to be mad at her. In fact, things got worse because I was unhappy. So I decided that I could choose to be a lot happier, and my mom and I could work things out. From that time on, I learned that being mad is only a feeling that goes away. The important thing is to work things out."

Obviously the content of your response to your child must be based on the specific situation, and on your child's capacity to understand. But even if you come up with a story that is not exactly relevant, the important thing is that you are relating to your child instead of dictating. Children love to hear that you were not perfect as a child, and that you felt the same things they feel. It helps your child grasp you as a person who knows what it is like to be a kid too. And children tend to remember "stories" from their parents' lives longer than they will remember straight-up advice.

Here are some examples of empathic responses that parents can make in reply to statements by their children. These are not scripts that you must use, but they might help you come up with your own responses down the road.

Child	Empathic Parent
"I really hate myself."	"I remember times when I wanted to paint myself black and hide in the dark. Is that what you mean?"
"I want to just run away."	"I feel that way right now too. I am so tired of how badly I have handled some things. Maybe you and I could go live in China right now."
"I want to burn the house down."	"That sounds like when I feel so mad and unappreciated I want to burn something. The house is a bit radical, but I want to burn off my frustration somehow."
"You are mean."	"Yes, I may seem mean sometimes because I have to do things that are not easy and say things I don't like to say. I'd rather be nice, but I have to be responsible as a mom."

Child	Empathic Parent
"You are being unfair."	"Let me tell you a story about when I was about your age. . . ."

FEEL IT AND THEN HEAL IT

Of all the therapeutic skills necessary for communication and resolution of problems, the ability to use empathy is one of the most important. This is as true for professional mental health workers as it is for parents. It may sound weird to focus on feelings before addressing the problems with actions, but it is critical to lay this groundwork for healing. Parents are naturally inclined to try to fix a child's problem first and ask questions later. There is nothing wrong with that, but it often is not the best response if you are looking for a long-term solution—and for a healthy, loving long-term relationship with your child. That's not to say that in some cases—such as a real emergency, when there is a physical threat to your child's safety—you shouldn't take action right away. But 99 percent of the time, it's better to approach your child's emotional distress with the goal of first understanding its roots, and then communicating that you are there for your child, with the child's best interests at heart.

Be warned that your child may surprise or even shock you when you probe for emotional context. I was wielding my empathic powers with great care upon a hostile six-year-old one day after he had turned on a teacher with a knife. Once he opened up, the boy informed me that he was trying to tell the teacher that he did not need her help because his father had told him, "Anytime someone helps you, they take some of your freedom away. They own you."

No wonder the child was acting out. It was his father's legacy.

Children are mysteries, just as we all are. We never fully understand them, just as we never quite understand ourselves. One of life's greatest delights, though, is discovering a few pieces of the puzzle—of your child and of yourself—as you live, work, play, and love together.

THE PLAN

Days 1–5

The following exercises will help sharpen your empathic skills and open the door to loving relationships. Create empathic responses for each of the scenarios. You need to expand these scenarios to ones you have experienced or anticipate. These exercises are intended to be used frequently, especially if you are having problems in communicating with your child.

- Your child comes in from school and is very upset because of a confrontation with a bully. "He was so big and mean. I was scared, but I didn't want him to know."

  Response 1:
  Response 2:
  Response 3:

- Your child just lied about doing homework when the teacher called. Your child says, "That old bag is a bad teacher, anyway."

  Response 1:
  Response 2:
  Response 3:

- You and your child are having a disagreement about going to bed. Your child says angrily: "You always tell me what to do. Who made you the boss?"

Response 1:
Response 2:
Response 3:

• Your child feels a best friend betrayed her: "She doesn't like me anymore. She'll tell everyone at school that I'm not her friend. I hate her."

Response 1:
Response 2:
Response 3:

• Your child is upset, but you don't know why. He is kicking things and saying, "I hate this. I hate this."

Response 1:
Response 2:
Response 3:

After you have spoken or recorded your empathic responses, it would be helpful to review them with your child, another child, another family member, a peer, or even a professional for additional possible responses. The concept is not to declare the *right* empathic response, but to add to and refine those you came up with. Listen to the feedback you get, and work to hone your empathic skills.

Professional therapists often describe scenarios and offer their empathic responses to sharpen their own skills. Then they will ask: "Do you think I was on the right feeling? How could I have said it better?" There is often a discussion of possible extenuating circumstances, followed by fresh scenarios. Empathic responses are discussed and recommended.

Don't be afraid to do these exercises with your child. You might find that you get some very honest and thoughtful responses. It might also lead to some interesting discussions about your child's own feelings. When you use imaginary situations to draw out your child's own thoughts and feelings, you are using a method known as "imagery resolution." This method often works because it gives your child some distance—and a sense of safety—from whatever the troubling real-life situation might be. This method can help resolve a conflict indirectly. It's the same philosophy behind the use of puppets and dolls in play therapy for children. When these playful objects are used to enact even painful scenarios, the child feels safer to talk about the feelings that are stirred.

Days 6–10

One of my most frequent tools for teaching families how to communicate their feelings is the Feelings Chart, developed by C. J. Lawlis (see page 96). This is an excellent tool for anyone in a family with children learning how to communicate with each other. Follow these steps:

1. Put the Feelings Chart in a central place, such as the refrigerator or on a corkboard. Each person gets a symbol, usually a magnet animal or taped symbol.
2. Each person indicates his feelings for the day on the chart so everyone can see. This creates a warning signal for those who are upset and need support.
3. At the dinner table (or other family meetings), each person discusses his feelings and how they emerged (such as reaction to another person's feelings or behavior.)
4. As the feelings are discussed, determine their source and what can be done to restore calm and security. For example, assume that a boy points to "anger" and tells how he felt mistreated by his father because he did not take him to the store as he promised. The family discusses what he can do about his feelings, and consider other feelings surrounding his anger, such as disappointment, frustration, and hurt. Action

steps are then considered, such as explaining his anger, disappointment, and so on to his dad (who is present), instead of pouting or isolating himself. This is news to the father, and after apologizing, he shares his own disappointment in the failed plans. This is a good lesson in how to resolve the negative feelings.

These discussions should be held at a designated time in which no distractions are present. It might be easier to space out these days so skills can be generalized and timing can be consistent with new issues.

FINAL NOTES

Communication is the key to problem solving in any relationship. Parents should never assume that they know what is going on with their children emotionally. Bonds of lasting love are created and strengthened when we reach out to ask, listen, and understand without judgment. Every child needs to be heard and understood. The better a parent is at providing a "safe place to land" for a child, the stronger the bonds.

9

Word Wise

This is the eighth segment in the 90-day program. It examines the power of the words parents use when talking to their children, and how miscommunications can occur. Parents will learn to choose words and use them in ways that prevent misunderstandings and conflicts. You have ten days, including two weekends, to complete this segment.

When I was working toward my master's degree at the University of North Texas, I became intrigued by the ways children respond to certain words and how their brains react to vowel sounds. One day while at the park with my son during that period, I overheard some mothers issuing commands to their children on the playground. I wrote down some of their instructions because I was struck by how confusing they must have been to the children.

"Hey! What are you doing? Whatever it is, stop it."

"Why are you shaking your leg like that? What are you thinking? If you are going to shake your leg like that, hit your hand."

"Hey, stop that. If I have to come out there, I am going to tear your arms off your body."

"Be nice. Be nice."

"Play! If you aren't going to play, we are going to leave."

"That was good, but you can do better. Do it again, but do it better."

"I don't know what is wrong with you."

"What are you doing? Do something else."

"Don't take that from him. Don't hit. Walk away. Run away."

"Don't cause trouble."

"Don't run. Watch out."

Admittedly, I've taken these statements out of context, but imagine how strange they must have sounded to the poor kids. Most parents are guilty of making similar statements from time to time. I have recordings of fathers "coaching" their kids at Little League games with instructions that must have left their kids wondering whether they were playing baseball or staging a life-and-death military operation.

Parents are often guilty of assuming that their children have bigger vocabularies and more advanced language skills than they do. No wonder we get so many blank stares and confused looks from our kids. Language skills are critical to your child's development. When I was studying French, German, and Spanish in college, one of my professors explained to me that the main problem was learning to *think* in different languages. Language can mold the brain's mechanics. Perhaps this is the reason certain cultures are known for specific skills, at least according to folklore. Germans have a very precise language, and it is a country renowned for its scientists, engineers, and precisely engineered products. Italian is an exuberant, passionate, and expressive language—is it a coincidence that their culture has produced so many of the world's great artists and performers?

The study of language and its effect on the brain is in its infancy, but we know that as a species we have the unique capacity to use imagery for self-reflection. We can also describe things and events that don't actually exist. We can imagine purple-dotted elephants or six-legged monsters and use language to make them real in our stories and films. Language and our extraordinary communications abilities have undoubtedly contributed to the success and dominance of our species.

PARENTS' COMPLEX COMMUNICATION

Human communication is incredibly complex, yet we often assume that our kids, whose language skills are still developing, understand everything we say to them. We can and do confuse our children when we fail to consider that our vocabularies, expressions, and manner of speaking may sometimes be over their heads and beyond their comprehension. Kevin brought in his five-year-old son, Jacob, because of wildly erratic behavior that he described as "schizo." One minute, Jacob was a very mellow, obedient child. The next, he was like a crazed animal, crawling on his hands and knees and even urinating in his pants.

His medical exams turned up nothing unusual, and his psychological tests were also within normal ranges. After $5,000 in tests, he still appeared to be a normal kid on paper. His school records were also unremarkable. In our interviews, I noted that he did not smile much, and he seemed nervous around his father. But in our two sessions, we played games designed to test his ability to handle stress, and he did just fine. Jacob never displayed any behavior I would label as schizophrenic when he was alone with me. It wasn't until I observed him work a puzzle with his father, in which they were supposed to combine their efforts to put it together, that I picked up on something unusual.

KEVIN: "I think you are a smart boy, but I need you to help me."
JACOB: "Dad, what can I do?"
KEVIN: "What do you mean—what do you do? You do what you're supposed to."
JACOB: "What am I supposed to do?"

KEVIN: "You are supposed to help me, and you are not."

JACOB: "Tell me how to help you, Dad, I don't know."

KEVIN (growing irritated): "That's the problem, isn't it? I always have to tell you what to do. You never can figure it out yourself."

JACOB (with tears in his eyes): "I really want to help you with this puzzle, and I have never done it before." (He starts looking at other toys and things in the room, obviously becoming distracted, and remains silent while his father becomes obsessed with the puzzle.)

KEVIN: "Jacob, what are you doing? Are you stupid, or just being uncooperative?"

(Jacob is confused by this question, as if he thinks that his dad really wants him to answer. He looks at me as if to say, "What should I do?" Then he panics and gets agitated.)

KEVIN (breaking the silence): "What the hell are you doing? Let's do this puzzle so we can get out of here."

At that point, Jacob displayed the behavior that his father had described. A glaze passed over his eyes. He became agitated and angry. He slapped himself and winced in pain. A wave of panic seemed to pass over him as he looked frantically for an exit. He ran toward the door, and then turned and ran back. It was disturbing behavior—the actions of a desperate and helpless creature in flight.

"You see, you see how crazy he is. I think I fathered a crazy kid," Kevin said.

Then the father began to cry in frustration and fear.

I went to Jacob, touched him on the shoulder, and gently rubbed his back and shoulders to comfort him. When he appeared to breathe more easily, I asked him to pick up a pencil on the floor.

Jacob slowly picked it up and gave it to me. I gave him an encouraging smile and said: "I have been looking all over the place for this pencil. Thank you so much for finding it and giving it back to me. This pencil means so much to me."

Jacob smiled back. "You're welcome," he said.

"Jacob, do you read?"

He nodded.

"Well, I have an eye problem today and can't focus my eyes very well. Could you read this and tell me what you think it says?"

I handed him a sheet of paper with instructions on how to install a new program on my computer.

We walked to my computer, and as he read the instructions, I went through the motions of installing the new program. We discussed how difficult it was to follow the instructions, but we muddled through and got the job done in just ten minutes. I offered to pay him for his assistance, which he accepted, much to my surprise. He was pleased with himself and, more important, back in control of his actions.

We rejoined Kevin and talked about what had happened earlier. I read to the father his own words to his son, and asked him what he meant by his remarks. It took several moments for the father to understand how his words were impacting his son. Finally we replayed the scenario in which I played his role and he played his son's, much to the delight of Jacob.

The father quickly got the point. It was no fun being his son. Jacob's bizarre behavior was a response to the stress his father put on him.

Many parents are unaware of the ways in which they express their own frustrations and anger in their communications with their children. But children are finely tuned receivers, and they will pick up on hostility and tensions that can have a very detrimental impact on their behavior. It turned out that Jacob's father resented the attention that his wife lavished on their son. The father admitted in later sessions that he had little patience with his son. He justified his cruel treatment by claiming that his son was a "momma's boy," and he was just trying to "make him a man."

Like most kids, Jacob wanted to please his parents. He wanted to love and be loved. He showed that in the way he had responded to my kinder words. But his father's disparaging words had Jacob so desperate that he acted out in frustration and confusion. His meltdowns would likely have continued into adulthood if his father had not seen the error of his ways and learned how to treat his son better.

ASSESSMENT

Are you unconsciously triggering similar reactions from your child? Do you make it easy for your child to love and be loved? Or are you constantly making your child work for your affections? This brief assessment is designed to provide insights:

- Does your child easily understand what you want or expect? This is not a yes-or-no answer. Ask your child if your desires are easy to understand. What words work? Does your child know what you really mean?
- Do you give your child options when you correct him, so he can find a way to please you? If your daughter is running around out of control, do you suggest ways that she can control herself and please you? "Try walking, honey."
- Do you allow your child to complete thoughts and sentences without interrupting? Do you insist on judging whatever is said? Do you jump ahead and anticipate the answer?
- Do you make assumptions about what your child is feeling without asking? Have you asked your child to share secrets with you?

- Do you use words and phrases that your child can easily understand, or do you sometimes confuse him? When you are talking to your child, ask him if he follows what you are saying.
- How do you encourage your child to be a team player? Do you teach your child, or do you make your child figure things out on her own?

SEVEN PARENTAL COMMUNICATION MISTAKES

In studies with children and adults alike, we use symbols in the form of words or numbers in our logical processing. If A = B and B = C, then does A = C? We pass information from one generation to the next in these forms, and our children learn cause and effect. For example, those who believe that cheating in sports or on tests is acceptable have had that lesson reinforced somewhere by someone they trusted. Parents also can pass on bad information without being aware of it, confusing their children and triggering defensive behaviors, even paralyzing them with helplessness.

Every child wants to please, to be loved and to love, but they can become confused about how to do those things if adults send them mixed or overly complex signals. In the worst cases, children react to their confusion and frustration with antisocial behavior. Here are the seven common mistakes parents make, confusing and frustrating their children instead of communicating with them.

1. The Double Bind

The double bind is a communicative situation where a person receives contradictory messages. The phrase *catch-22* is sometimes used to describe double-bind situations, also known as "no-win situations." A catch-22 situation, like a double bind, is also inherently self-defeating: the very act of trying to solve it prevents it from happening.

The essence of a double bind is two conflicting demands, neither of which can be ignored, which leaves the hearer torn and conflicted. There is no way to win because both demands cannot be met. "I must do it but I can't do it" is a typical description of the double-bind experience. It demands that the child find a way to resolve what is (to the child) an unsolvable, yet unavoidable problem.

The contradictory message often comes from a parent, grandparent, or older sibling. A mother might give an order that directly conflicts with one given by a father, or a teacher. The child does not want to disobey either, but to obey one is to defy the other. No wonder the poor kid acts out in frustration and fear.

EXAMPLES OF THE DOUBLE BIND

- Have you stopped beating your little brother yet? (The implication that the question *must* receive a yes or no answer creates a double bind.)
- A sign saying, "Do Not Read This Sign."
- A parent who tells a child to question the authority of the government, other family members, and school officials with an instruction like, "Don't let them run your life." (When we question authority, we are forced to acknowledge the primacy of that authority.)
- A child is taunted for being shy to the point that he yells in frustration. Then the child is spanked for the outburst. The child learns two contradictory messages: I must express myself to be accepted, and I must not express myself in order to be accepted.

2. The "But" Kick

Consider these sentences:

"I think you are a good boy, but you are not being good now."
"You did a good job, but you messed up here."
"I really think you are smart, but you made a stupid mistake."

The word *but* is used here as an adjunctive condition as well as an afterthought, but the psychological message is 90 percent based on the information following the *but*.

What the child hears from that sentence is, "You are not good, you messed up, and you are stupid." This sentence structure confuses the child and makes him think that the parent's love is conditional rather than unconditional.

It sounds rather simple, but instead of using *but,* substitute the word *and,* which unites the two ideas in the sentence. Consider these modifications of the earlier statements and see how different the messages feel:

"I think you are a good boy, and you are not being good now."
"You did a good job, and you messed up here."
"I really think you are smart, and you made a stupid mistake."

The use of the word *and* instead of *but* allows the brain of the child to comprehend the point of comparison in these appraisals. When I change this single word in therapy sessions, children respond positively in every case. They get the full meaning, and the positive message doesn't get buried by the negative one.

3. No Positive Direction

Children become confused when you give them vague orders without direction. Often this happens when parents fail to put action verbs in sentences such as:

"Be nice."

"Be careful."

"Don't be rude."

"Don't be ugly."

"Be sweet."

"Don't be a pain in the neck."

"Don't be a problem."

"Don't look like you're stupid."

"Do look smart."

"Make me proud of you."

If you look closely, you will not see one action verb in all of these sentences. They tell a child how to be, not what to *do*. For example, how do you *be* nice? You can act in nice ways, you can perform nice functions, you can even have a nice attitude, but these are all actions. We have to know what actions to do in order to be perceived as being nice by other people.

You have to tell children what to do, not what to be. They are already being something—themselves. If you want to tell them how to treat you, you have to use action verbs. If you want your child to act in specific ways so you can label her as "nice," then the observed behaviors you want to see have to be articulated.

When I was about five years old, my grandfather told me to be "stout." To this day, I have never understood what that meant in action. I tried to be strong and demonstrated I could do vast amounts of work, but he never praised me as being "stout" when I performed. I tried to be brave and courageous, standing up for justice and fair treatment, yet he never praised me for being stout. In fact, I never knew what the heck being "stout" meant to him.

I had a friend, Troy, who had a similar problem. His father always told him not to be "classy." His father would say, "If you get classy, I will whip your butt." I asked him what that meant, and he admitted he had no idea, except that it meant that he was not acting right. I guess he never was classy, because I never heard that he got punished for it, but he sure worried a lot that he might do something "classy" and get his butt whipped.

4. Abuse of Trust

Many parents have confessed to me that they take joy in making their children work hard for approval. Some even punish them when they fail. This is a cruel and dangerous game. It just doesn't dawn on many parents that they are playing with the minds and emotions of their children when they withhold approval. This is a great way to confuse and frustrate children until they explode with anger. Children who feel they can never please their parents suffer from poor self-esteem that can cripple them emotionally in adulthood. Children initially measure their worth by their ability to please their parents. When the parents withhold their approval and their love, they play a dangerous game that will likely end in rebellion, or worse. By the age of ten, children who are treated that way will stop trying to please such parents—and then things will get really ugly.

When parents withhold approval and affection, they give up the most powerful currency they have for motivating their children and for building long-term, loving bonds. Don't make that mistake. Be clear with your child about what it takes to please and displease you. Give them boundaries and guidelines that they can live with. It's not difficult to do that:

"When you make your own breakfast, it makes me proud of you."
"I expect you to clean up after yourself like a big girl."

Your responsibility as a parent is to help your child thrive by giving her guidelines and encouraging her to live within them. If you don't do that, it is not the child's fault. It is yours.

5. The Question-Answer Quandary

CHILD: "Can I go over to Billy's and play?"
PARENT: "Why do you want to know?"
CHILD: "Because he has some new computer. Can I go?"
PARENT: "How did he get the new computer?"
CHILD: "I guess his parents bought it for him. Can I go?"
PARENT: "What kind is it?"
CHILD: "I don't know. Can I go?"
PARENT: "Then why do you want to see it?"

Now I have a question: Do you want your child to become a raving lunatic? Then follow that formula. Never give a straight answer to your child's straightforward question. Then stand back and wait for the poor kid to lash out or give up in frustration. Parents who play this game destroy the child's effort at two-way communication. The payback will come later. When you shut off communication to your child by failing to respond to questions, there will come a time when the child simply stops asking. Then, the parent is the one left without a clue.

6. Tuned Out

It is not always easy for parents to focus and pay full attention when a child talks to them. Adults tend to juggle a variety of jobs and tasks that compete for our attention. But our children need us to tune in to them. Often, their words are less important than the emotions behind them, but you need to help your children express their thoughts by engaging in conversations with them that follow through on their interests and questions. If your child starts talking about her day in school or what questions she has in life, help her express her thoughts without being sidetracked.

Consider this conversation between a parent and child:

SON: "My friends and I were talking about how mothers and daddies really get together and have a family. How did you and Dad start our family?"

MOM: "Well, we met at a party and it went from there. It was so long ago."

SON: "Did you kiss and stuff like that?"

MOM: "Sure. Why are you asking me about this? Are you up to something with a girl already?"

SON: "No, I just wanted to know . . ."

MOM: "Frankly, it is none of your business, but I will tell you what your business is. If I ever catch you doing something with a girl, I am going to tear your arms off."

This may be an extraordinary example, but it shows how parents can thwart a child's effort to have a conversation. It not only frustrates the child, it hinders his ability to follow a stream of thought. This is what I call "schizophrenic" talk because it disrupts the flow of conversation. Further, it can create a neurological pattern that disrupts a child's ability to concentrate, triggering attention deficit disorder.

7. Mind-Shattering

Consider the following dialogue:

MOM: "I saw you trying to get that toy from your little brother. What do you have to say for yourself?"

CHILD: "I was not going to keep it. He wasn't playing with it, and I wanted to see it. I didn't mean to take it and keep it."

MOM: "When were you going to give it back to him? Why didn't you ask me?"

CHILD: "I don't know. I wasn't gonna do anything with it."

MOM: "You know what I think? I think you were going to steal that toy from your brother because you don't like your brother much, do you? You are really jealous of him, and you want everything he wants, so you are a self-centered little kid."

"Mind-shattering" is when you hijack someone's feelings with your own interpretation and demean them. In this case, the child might have had jealous feelings, but the mother's quick condemnation of the child as "self-centered" only shames him, darkening his self-image without guiding him toward more positive actions.

I've had thousands of clients tell me of similar incidents and how hurtful these were for them as children. It takes only a few seconds to damage a child's self-image, but repeated incidents can do a lifetime of hurt. None of us have the right to hurt those who depend on us for help and guidance.

SEVEN "TO-DO" METHODS
FOR POSITIVE PARENTAL COMMUNICATION

Here are methods that parents can use to improve their communications with their children and bring them closer by expressing expectations clearly and without judgment:

1. Be Clear

You can express what you want and expect from your child without making harsh judgments. You don't need to sugarcoat either. It is even okay sometimes to raise your voice and let your child know that you are frustrated with bad behavior, as long as you don't say hurtful things. I was trying to get my kids ready for school one day, and it was chaos. Shoes were lost. Socks lacked mates. Cereal was spilled. Homework disappeared. Kids crying. You know the drill. (I'm recommending legislation that would allow parents of schoolchildren to report for work in pajamas dripping with Cheerios and milk.)

Finally, I had my own little meltdown: "I am so frustrated I could yell! And so I am! Arrrrrrrrrrrrgh!"

Silence from the peanut gallery. It took them a second or two to decide that Daddy hadn't really lost his mind. Then they cracked up. *Daddy lost it!*

I yelled again. And they joined me, laughing with me.

Tension dissolved.

"Okay, Dad, we get your point," the oldest said.

Order was restored in the Lawlis universe.

My meltdown was not a calculated move in behavior modification. No, I *really* had a meltdown. But I wasn't lashing out at my children. I was expressing my frustration clearly. And they got it, without being harangued or threatened—and because we all laughed about "Daddy's meltdown," it actually drew us closer. My children responded with humor and sympathy and then tried to calm me by getting themselves ready for school. Believe it or not, kids get it when you make yourself clear.

I'm not advocating that parents use the primal screams to control their children, but it is okay for your kids to understand that you are human, that their actions can frustrate you. Again, honesty and directness are great tools.

I once watched a mother in a department store try to control her daughter, who was swinging on the clothes racks. She grabbed the girl's arm, and the child went into her own crying meltdown: "Mommy, are you mad at me? Are you ashamed of me? Am I a bad girl?"

The mother, who noticed that I was watching, forced a smile and replied: "No, Mommy is not mad at you. You are my sweetie-pie. But you need to be good and stay close to Mommy. You are just playing, but please don't do that again."

It was a nice try, but the mother had just given her child license to keep tearing up the joint. A better response would have been, "I am not mad at you, but I am very frustrated, and it stresses me out when you climb on the clothes. Will you make Mommy happier by not climbing on the clothes? Help me decide what to buy you instead."

That is a more direct and honest response, and it gives the child better options.

2. Give Cause-and-Effect Directions

Kids like to know they have power, so let them know that their actions affect you—especially when they make you happy. My father came to me when I was six years old and told me that he was proud of me because someone saw me help an elderly neighbor sweep off her porch after a snowfall. I didn't remember doing it—it might not have been me—but from that point on I never missed an opportunity to help a neighbor. Pleasing my father meant a great deal to me.

3. Own Your Feelings

If your child's behavior is annoying or stressing you, take owner-ship of those feelings instead of issuing commands. Rather than say-ing, "You are acting like a jackass, settle down," try this: "I'm getting irritated by your crazy behavior. Settle down before I send you to bed early."

By using yourself as the reference point, you let your child know that the crazy behavior is having an impact on you. This empowers them to do something that makes you feel better, and kids generally respond well when given that choice.

4. Make Directions Simple

Research into mental processes finds that the average adult human brain can manage an average of seven "bits" of information at one time. (A bit is a type of information, like a number or sym-bol.) Under optimal conditions, the average person can handle nine

bits. That is the reason telephone numbers are usually seven numbers, and car license tags use less than eight.

Parents need to keep the limits of the brain in mind when giving
directions to their children, who often are so distracted that their
ability to process information is more limited. They respond best to
one-step instructions. You likely won't get a satisfactory response if
you pile one order upon another, telling a child to get some socks,
make sure they are clean, then put on brown shoes, and pick up the
dirty clothes on the way out of the bedroom.

Keep it simple and limit the number of steps so your child can
focus on the essentials. And above everything else, use words that
your child understands. When my father was teaching me how to
drive a stick shift, he kept telling me to put it in "high" gear. I took
that to mean "higher in the air." So I shoved the stick shift upward,
grinding the gears every time.

5. Wrap Lessons in Stories

The Greeks used fables. The Brothers Grimm had their fairy tales.
The Bible offers parables. Parents should be storytellers too. Your
children are more likely to learn a lesson if it is wrapped in an enter-
taining story—especially one in which they play a role—that engages
their minds. If you tell your child that being selfish will drive friends
away, it is doubtful that the lesson will stick. But if you offer the
same lesson in the context of a story, the odds are better that they'll
get it: "Do you remember when you were at the country fair, and
you shared your cotton candy with your friends? They were so grateful, one little girl even gave you a kiss! Just think, if you had eaten it
all yourself and not shared, you would have missed that."

It can be hard to think of good stories to make points, so I advise
parents to prepare a bit by compiling a list of stories that effectively
communicate what you want your child to know on important top-
ics such as: love, honesty, frustration, generosity, friendship, loyalty,
selfishness, pride, thoughtfulness, temptation, and leadership.

6. Ask for Feedback

Parents find it very enlightening to get feedback on their communications with their children. You can solicit feedback with questions such as:

"What do I say when I am mad or angry?"
"What do I say when I am happy?"
"What do I say that makes you feel bad about yourself?"
"What do I say that makes you feel the best about yourself?"
"What do I say that lets you know I love you?"
"What other words do you like to hear me say?"
"What do you think I mean when I use these words?"

7. Check Up on Your Communication Skills

Record your conversations with your children and later listen carefully to your word choices and tone of voice. Are you using words they understand? Are your instructions simple and clear?

When imparting lessons with stories, parents need to make sure the point isn't lost in the details. I realized this while telling my child a story about a lost little girl who used her smarts to find her way home by looking for directional signs like the position of the sun, smoke from the factories near her home, and other sources. After my in-depth tale, I asked my daughter what she learned from the story. "I learned that if I ever get lost, I'd like to have that smart little girl with me."

THE PLAN

Days 1–4

Keep a journal of all the conversations you have had, especially the difficult ones. Try to remember and jot down the words and how you used them. Study the words you and your family use to communicate your needs and instructions. Take some time and have a discussion with your child and others as to what you meant and what they intended to communicate with the words on your list.

Days 5–10

For each day of this process, complete the following steps:

- Decide on a mutual topic to discuss. It can be a conflict that hasn't been resolved, a philosophical topic (like the values you hold high for the family or God), an issue that you find irritating, or whatever you want to have a dialogue about with your child or other family member.
- Take exactly ten minutes for both of you to write down your thoughts and perceptions or what you think should be done. Writing out thoughts is good for children, even if they come up with only a sentence.
- Take exactly ten minutes to accomplish the following steps:
  1. Each of you take turns and read aloud the other's letter.
  2. Try to use your own words to explain what you believe the other person's letter meant.
  3. Get confirmation of your explanation or clarification from the other person. Example: "I thought your letter said that you thought I was being unclear in how I asked for your help with cleaning the house. Is that right?" Response: "No, I just wanted to know what you expected of me so I could plan other things to do rather than just doing everything you think of."
  4. With the clarification, state your response. (This can lead into a discussion, but be sure you finish this step within the ten-minute limit.)
- Following the structured interaction, have a five-minute discussion of how you two felt about the process and outcome.

FINAL NOTES

Across all cultures, humans express love for each other in words as well as actions. Sometimes we convey those feelings in poetry and in music too. Yet finding the right words to deepen relationships does not come easily to those of us who are not orators, poets, or great lyricists. That's okay. You can learn the words and phrases that touch your children and draw them closer, but you have to feel them from your own heart and soul if you want them to be believed and trusted.

When I work with dying patients, I often ask them to tell me their life stories because it helps bring meaning to their final hours. This is a very fulfilling time for both of us, because all of us live our lives as stories. Nearly all of the stories I've heard include lessons—good and bad—that were learned from the person's parents. Your children will not forget your examples and guidance, both good and bad.

One person said, "My father looked at me in the eye and said, 'You are a curse to me.' I will never forget that." He died with that tragic thought still lodged in his mind, even though he had been a church pastor for more than fifty years and had served his community in very distinguished roles. In his town of 5,000 people, more than 1,000 came to his funeral because he had been not a curse but a blessing to them. Still, his father's words followed him to his grave.

Another individual said, "My mother told me that she would always love me, even after she died. I believed her and still do."

How will your words be remembered?

I am always amused, and sometimes mortified, when my grown children tell me what they remember of my parenting. I am humbled by their forgiveness for my misguided statements, and I can only pray that they know the love that I have for them in my heart, even when I fail to communicate it adequately.

There is an old philosophical question that every psychologist in training has to answer. If a tree falls in the forest, and no one is there to hear it, does it make a sound? The answer is that there would be no sound because sound is only the sensations of air vibrations in our ears. If no one is there to "hear" the vibrations, they remain only as vibrations in the air.

Words are only vibrations, and mean nothing if no one hears them. But when they are heard, they can have powerful and lasting impacts. Be careful of what you say to your children. Hurting or healing, your words will follow them for a lifetime.

10

Forgiveness and Renewal

This is the ninth segment in the 90-day program. It deals with the power of forgiveness and the poisonous effect that its lack can have on your relationship with your child. This may prove to be a challenging section, but the rewards will be worth it. Because this segment requires great insight and courage, you are allotted fifteen days to complete it.

It happens so often. I'll be deep into a therapy session with an adult client suffering from severe depression or addiction, and the root of his complex and debilitating problem will suddenly be revealed. He was beaten. He was belittled. He was abandoned. He was sexually assaulted.

These are serious and hurtful wrongs that no person should have had to endure. Yet all can be forgiven, not for the good of the wrongdoer but for that of the victim. It comes down to this: Things will happen to you that are beyond your control. But you can control how you respond to them. You can accept the role of victim and take on all that goes with it: depression, bitterness, addiction, and misery. Or you can move onward and upward by practicing self-preservation with forgiveness.

After years of treating "victims," I've come to suspect that the root of all suffering emanates from this one source—the inability to practice forgiveness. Learning to forgive is a critical survival skill.

Life will slap you upside the head. Indignities, insults, hurts, injustices, and attacks will assault you. None of us goes through life unscathed. And there is not one of us who has not hurt someone, either intentionally or otherwise. As parents, we make mistakes and our children suffer. Our children will make mistakes that hurt us. For the sake of our long-term relationships, we need to forgive each other and move on. Know that, and practice it daily, if necessary.

When Oscar's parents brought him to see me, they hit my office like a rolling street brawl. The father, Nick, announced that they needed my help with their "problem son." Oscar had hooked up with a gang. In loud and angry tones, his father listed the boy's offenses at school and around town. It was a substantial list that included burglary, theft, truancy, and resisting arrest.

The kid was only fifteen years old, but Oscar had the gangbanger look down. He oozed the menace of a street thug twice that age. He had dragon tattoos on both arms and wore his hair in a greasy ponytail. Black jeans. Black T-shirt. Black boots, and a black leather jacket that reeked of cigarette smoke. He had the bling too, heavyweight champion silver jewelry on his fingers and wrists.

By contrast, the little thug's father looked like a high school track coach or a decathlon champ who stepped off a box of Wheaties. Jogging suit, tennis shoes, short haircut, white T-shirt. No bling. No tattoos. But the powerful scent of his cologne nearly made my eyes water, as if he was overcompensating for something foul in the air.

His mother, Ana, was all but invisible in the presence of these two strong and competing males. She spoke in a faint voice and wore a nondescript business suit. She kept her arms folded and her handbag in her lap.

The father pulled his chair directly in front of mine so he could hold my attention. Oscar and his mom took the couch. The family power structure was thus made clear. I interrupted Nick as he continued his account of the boy's sins.

"Oscar, I've heard what you've done to upset your parents. What have they done to you that caused you to do these things?"

At first, the boy was shocked. He remained silent, mulling over this twist. He'd been prepared to be the accused, not the accuser. Finally he said, "Nothing. They have done nothing that made me do what I did. I don't know what you mean."

Dad didn't like the new line of questioning at all.

"You can't pin his crimes on us. He did them. If you are trying to blame us, we are done with you, Dr. Lawlis."

My response was low-key and deliberate.

"Nick, is your approach to parenting working for you? Is it making things better? I guess if it is, then maybe you should keep it up. I won't be one bit offended if you go to someone else who tells you what you want to hear. Thanks for coming in."

I got up from my chair and extended my hand to Oscar and his mother, but Nick did not accept the invitation to leave. This intense guy did not give up that easily when challenged.

Finally he said, "Okay, Doc. Maybe I jumped the gun. Let's give this a try."

I suggested that Nick and I talk privately. Once we were alone, I told him that if I was going to help them, he would have to follow my lead and trust in my expertise and experience.

Nick's demeanor changed dramatically. "I am just so embarrassed by what has happened. I want it to go away. I look like an incompetent parent with a thug for a son. I think he is doing this to hurt me. And when you asked him to tell you *my* mistakes, I couldn't handle it." With that, he buried his face in his hands and began to breathe very deeply, as if he were trying to keep from fainting. Then he began to sob. He wept for ten minutes as if his heart were breaking.

Finally he began to whisper, "Why did he do this to me? Why does he hate me so much to do this?"

I asked Nick to explain those statements to me.

"My son. Can't you see it? He is making a fool out of me, with his stupid clothes and punk look. He makes me look like a failure and a fool."

I told the father that he seemed to have a very set idea of what his son should be. "It sounds like you can't forgive him for not being what you wanted," I said. "I'm sure he senses your disappointment."

Nick's attitude underwent another rapid transformation. He sprang to his feet, wiped his eyes, and glared, jabbing a finger at me.

"You expect me to forgive him for what he has done to me? Don't you understand what I have had to do all my life? I was just a poor Mexican kid who had to drink river water and eat beans and tortillas every day. But since I was athletic and worked my butt off, I earned respect. I have never stopped working and fighting for respect. Now my own son is destroying my reputation. He is dragging me down with him." He shook with anger, but finally dropped back into his chair, emotionally exhausted.

I told Nick that I understood his perspective, but offered that maybe he should consider his son's point of view too.

Nick shrugged passively, so I asked Oscar to come into the room. The sight of his father hunched over in his chair clearly worried him.

"Tell me, what is it like to be your father's son?"

It took him a couple of minutes to decide it was safe to respond. Then it poured out of him.

"I used to want to be just like him. I wanted to be a jock like him so he'd be proud of me. Then one morning, I didn't get ready for a workout as fast as he wanted, so he left without me, saying, It won't do you any good anyway. He let me know that I would never measure up."

It was the son's turn to shut down.

I finished Oscar's story for him. "So you decided to get even by doing things that would embarrass and hurt your father? And you succeeded, right?"

Tears rolled down his cheeks, but the tough kid didn't cry. He studied his father, trying to figure out how he would react. He didn't get the response he'd expected.

Nick reached out for him.

"I'm sorry. I didn't mean that. I was trying to motivate you. It was wrong. Please forgive me."

For the first time, this father and son were connecting. I left them for a few minutes. When I returned, they were still in an embrace.

"Have you two decided to forgive each other?"

As they nodded, I added another instruction.

"Exactly what are you forgiving, and how are you going to treat each other differently? You first, Dad."

Nick stammered, "I don't like the gangbanging or the way you've acted, Oscar. But I will always love you as my son."

Oscar was overwhelmed.

"Dad, I forgive you for putting me down. It still hurts, but even so, I will always love you too."

I then asked them where they wanted to go from that point. "What sort of relationship would you like to have?"

We had work to do. In the sessions that followed, I helped them get through the hurts and disappointments. They discussed their personal needs and what they could do for each other. They exchanged bitter words at times, but eventually they made peace. They were both ambitious and intelligent, and they knew they were hurting each other.

I told Nick that he was emotionally stunted and helped him work through his own issues. Oscar came around quickly, showing uncommon wisdom once he got over his quest for revenge. Eventually he dropped the gangbanger act, went out for football, and became a star.

The circumstances underlying that family conflict are not unusual. Parents and children give each other ample opportunity to practice forgiveness. Too often, family members choose bitterness, revenge, and self-destructive behaviors instead of embracing the simple principle of forgiveness. I see it time and again, and it usually begins with one of the following issues:

TOP TEN REASONS CITED BY UNFORGIVING PARENTS

Bitterness and conflict result when a child:

1. Does not meet high expectations academically.
2. Is not as attractive as the parents.
3. Creates social problems for the parents.
4. Does not resemble one of the parents.
5. Has different interests than the parents.
6. Comes between the parents.
7. Is ill and demands great attention.
8. Behaves abnormally and cannot be controlled.
9. Has talent or beauty that attracts more attention than the parents can handle.
10. Disappoints the parents.

It works both ways, of course.

TOP TEN REASONS CITED BY UNFORGIVING CHILDREN

Children often act out or go underground when parents:

1. Do not listen or try to understand their problems.
2. Let their own lives take precedence over the family.
3. Love another child more.
4. Work all the time and are never around.
5. Take no pride in the child's accomplishments.

6. Are divorced.
7. Smother the child, allowing no freedom.
8. Are alcoholics and/or drug abusers.
9. Are irresponsible.
10. Are too strict.

THE TOLL OF AN UNFORGIVING HEART

Forgiveness is the act of separating emotions from actions that have caused hurt. To forgive does not mean that hurtful actions were justified. It doesn't make a wrong right, or a bad act good. That is often a difficult concept for people to grasp, and it's understandable. A woman who was raped as a child may balk at forgiving her rapist. It is an evil, despicable, and cruel act. It is wrong. But in forgiving the person, she doesn't change any of that. She only removes the emotions so that she can heal and move on.

The same holds true for someone with an unfaithful spouse. It is possible to forgive, and heal, without condoning the act itself. The cheating will not be forgotten. The scar is still there, but healing can occur with forgiveness. Forgiveness is the removal of the fear and anger around the injury. It is not a lobotomy. The memory remains.

The key point is that forgiveness benefits the forgiver; it doesn't clear the offender. When the victim refuses to forgive, that person remains a victim—and what good is there in being a victim? Holding on to anger and shame only poisons your psychological and physiological health. The emotional turmoil feeds on itself and builds into obsessive behaviors.

I've seen it in my own family. My mother built up tremendous hatred of her stepmother. It surfaced any time she talked about her. Even though she grew up in an affluent family with a nanny and servants, she was bitter about never receiving enough maternal attention. She looked upon her childhood with disgust and shame until her dying day. She took her unforgiving heart to her grave, and probably died sooner than she might have if she had only focused instead on the blessings in her life.

A lack of forgiveness truly can be harmful to your health. Unresolved anger triggers hormonal activity that produces chemical imbalances. High blood pressure, muscle tension, and unhealthy blood cell counts result from the stress. My mother had severe arthritis, heart disease, and stomach ulcers that might have been alleviated had she only practiced forgiveness toward her stepmother.

It's bad enough to let your anger and bitterness consume you, but it can also destroy your ability to form lasting, loving relationships. The saddest situation I see is when parents and children are torn apart even though they desperately want to connect. The loss of love can be deadly. I have watched family relationships ripped apart over blatantly stupid and meaningless things. One mother and daughter were alienated for twenty years because of a conflict that began over what color the daughter's bedroom was to be painted. The mother died without reconciliation, compounding the tragedy.

I've lost loved ones over the years, and it exasperates me when I see people take time for granted, thinking wounds will heal eventually. Don't count on that. Practice forgiveness while you still have the chance. Heal the wounds and rebuild the bonds. The price of bitterness and anger is too high for both of you. It takes far more courage to forgive than it does to wallow in victimization.

Often, people have unrealistic expectations of relationships, and they let the slightest perceived insult or thoughtless act destroy bonds. Parents should expect that their children will disappoint them in some way at some point. Children need to understand that parents are human, and they mess up. Count on it. And be ready to forgive and move on. The rewards of a lifelong loving bond will make it worth your while.

Forgiveness issues come up in psychotherapy more than any other matter. I have developed specific exercises for helping clients forgive others so that they can heal and move forward. Often, it helps to do these with another person.

THE PLAN: DAYS 1–7

The old saying, "Forgive and forget," may sound like a great idea, but it is easier said than done when you have been deeply hurt, abused, or grievously harmed. Letting go and moving on may be the hardest thing you will ever do. But do you really want to live with anger and bitterness as a constant companion? This set of exercises will take you through the forgiving process. Take time to think about your answers, talk about the feelings they bring up, and reflect on what they mean for you as a parent.

Step One: Know What Needs to Be Forgiven

Until you can forgive someone who has hurt you, the emotional pain will keep you in a cycle of reliving the pain. Halting that cycle is reason enough to forgive. Your approach shouldn't be to say: "From now on, it never happened." Instead, think of it as "letting go" so that you can enjoy life. Think about things in your life that still need to be forgiven. You can be sure that whatever it is, it's holding you back.

What do you need to forgive of a:

- Parent or guardian? (Examples: Abuse, neglect, unreasonable expectations, lack of affection, irresponsible parenting.)

_____

_____

_____

- Sibling? (Examples: Bullying, lying, stealing, ignoring you.)

_____

_____

_____

• Former lover or spouse? (Examples: Cheating, finding someone else, lying, abuse.)

_____

_____

_____

• Friend? (Examples: Not living up to expectations, lying, ignoring you.)

_____

_____

_____

What do you need to forgive in your child?

• Does not meet high expectations academically.
• Is not attractive.
• Creates social problems.
• Has different interests.
• Comes between us as parents.
• Is ill and demands great attention.
• Behaves abnormally and cannot be controlled.
• Has talent or beauty that attracts more attention than you can
  handle.
• Disappoints you.
• Does not match the academic success expected for the family
  background.

_____

_____

_____

You might also want to consider what your child needs to forgive you for:

- Deserting him—physically or emotionally.
- Divorcing/remarrying.
- Not understanding him.
- Being harsh.
- Being lax.
- Being absent when he needed you.
- Adopting him.
- Forcing beliefs on him.
- Frightening him.
- Being abusive.
- Failing to provide.
- Loving another child more.
- Working too much away from home.
- Not being proud of his achievements.
- Loving him too much.
- Being an addictive personality.
- Not being responsible, and allowing something bad to happen.
- Letting a sibling bully him.

_____

_____

_____

Step Two: Recognize the Effects of Not Forgiving

You have just identified hurts that you have not forgiven. As painful as this process may be, it gives you the opportunity to free yourself and to grow as an individual and in your relationships. Holding on to past hurts has a direct, and often escalating, effect on the relationship between the victim and the offender. The closer the relationship, the more damaging that lack of forgiveness is likely to be.

You and your child should separately pick the three most significant hurts in Step One that continue to cause pain. Record each one below, along with how long you have held on to that particular hurt. Write a sentence or two that describes where that relationship is now. Then share what you've written with one another (optional).

Unforgiven event: How long have you held on to the pain?

_____   _____

Describe how it affects your relationship today.

_____

Unforgiven event: How long have you held on to the pain?

_____   _____

Describe how it affects your relationship today.

_____

Unforgiven event: How long have you held on to the pain?

_____   _____

Describe how it affects your relationship today.

_____

You have just completed an important assessment of how your relationships have changed because you refused to forgive. It's also important to understand the feelings that arise from that refusal. With your child, go through the lists below and separately check any conditions that regularly affect you. Then share your lists and discuss how these feelings relate to past hurts.

Parent:

____ Sadness   ____ Automatic dislike of
____ Lack of trust   strangers
____ Sense of helplessness   ____ Fear of failure
____ Nervousness   ____ Cynicism
____ Anger   ____ Self-defeating choices
____ Headaches   ____ Fear of intimacy

____ Anxiety
____ Unwillingness to accept help
____ Fear of commitment
____ Low motivation
____ Drug dependence
____ Sick feelings
____ Reluctance to change
____ Trouble with authority

____ Envy
____ Insomnia
____ Oversensitivity
____ Sense of isolation
____ Hopelessness
____ Panic attacks
____ Sense of dread
____ Other: _____

Child:

____ Sadness
____ Lack of trust
____ Sense of helplessness
____ Nervousness
____ Anger
____ Headaches
____ Anxiety
____ Unwillingness to accept help
____ Fear of commitment
____ Low motivation
____ Drug dependence
____ Sick feelings
____ Reluctance to change
____ Trouble with authority

____ Automatic dislike of strangers
____ Fear of failure
____ Cynicism
____ Self-defeating choices
____ Fear of intimacy
____ Envy
____ Insomnia
____ Oversensitivity
____ Sense of isolation
____ Hopelessness
____ Panic attacks
____ Sense of dread
____ Other: _____

Review the following sentences separately and check any that may describe you when the going gets tough in a relationship. Be as honest as you can about these. You can't grow until you know where you are.

You:

_____ I disappear into my "cave."

_____ I freak out.

_____ I cry too much.

_____ I fly off the handle.

_____ I deliver the silent treatment.

_____ I act superior.

_____ I belittle the other person.

_____ I make jokes.

_____ I turn intellectual.

_____ I resort to alcohol or drugs.

_____ I place blame on others.

_____ I break things.

Your child (optional):

_____ I withdraw.

_____ I freak out.

_____ I cry too much.

_____ I get angry.

_____ I deliver the silent treatment.

_____ I make jokes.

_____ I do whatever I have to do to please the other person.

_____ I turn cynical.

_____ I call in reinforcements (friends, family, etc.).

_____ I place blame on others.

_____ I break things.

_____ I yell.

_____ I cling.

Step Three: Share the Feelings behind Your Reactions

It is important to recognize the negative feelings that you carry around like old baggage. Once you do that, put a name to each feeling. This will help you move beyond it. Go back to Step One and review your list of unforgiven hurts. Then you and your child each choose five of the items you checked and record them below. For each item, answer the question: "What about it caused the pain?" Another way to look at the question is to ask, "What did it *mean* to you?" or, "How did it make you feel about yourself?"

You:

1. _____

I felt _____

2. _____

I felt _____

3. _____

I felt _____

4. _____

I felt _____

5. _____

I felt _____

Your child (optional):

1. _____

I felt _____

2. _____

I felt _____

3. _____

I felt _____

4. _____

I felt _____

5. _____

I felt _____

You have just identified the feelings that gave you so much pain; yet you haven't forgiven the person who caused them. Now you both have the crucial information you need to begin the process of letting go.

Step Four: Talk about It

The process of forgiveness requires that you let go of a negative feeling. If you've held on to the feeling for any length of time, it has become not only familiar, but habitual. Letting it go leaves an emotional vacuum that you may be tempted to fill with similar feelings, so it's important to choose healthier feelings (freedom, release, peace, gratitude, weightlessness, self-esteem, and so on) to replace it with. One productive way to do this is to join with your child and create an emotional experience that replaces the old pain with a more positive emotion that carries the same wallop.

We all have stories about how things that were said at one time in our lives linger way past the context, the pain continuing for years. Most of these stories relate to the tumultuous periods during a child's early teenage years. Their hormone-driven rebelliousness and instinctual drive for independence makes kids perceive parents as anchors around their necks. Teens can be unconsciously hurtful at this stage because they tend to think of adults as holding all the power. I know of a father who was deeply hurt when his sixteen-year-old daughter told him that he was a failure as a parent and she never wanted to see him again. She said he smelled bad and embarrassed her friends with his stupid jokes. These words were the typical thoughtless talk that is only meant to convey powerlessness, but this father made the mistake of listening to the words instead of the emotions. The father carried that pain in his heart for twenty years, until one day he asked if his daughter still felt that way. She didn't even remember saying such things, but she was wise enough to beg his forgiveness. She assured him that he was a great father and that she never intended to hurt him. Her healing words meant far more to her father than she could fathom.

Have a look at the list of hurts you compiled in Step Four. Take turns discussing each of the items you and your child listed, then decide on a method for letting go of the feelings you've identified so that you can replace them. You might write the negative and positive feelings on separate pieces of paper. Put the negative feelings in the fireplace and burn them up, or place them in a bag and throw them in the trash. As you do that, take the substitute feelings and place them in your pocket or in a special box. Whenever you're tempted to return to the negative, repeat the ritual. Record the ritual you choose here, then apply it to each of the hurts you recorded in Step Four.

Ritual for forgiveness:

_____

_____

_____

Now that you've created a specific way to act out your decision to forgive, you're ready to put it into action.

Step Five: Put It to Work

You should understand now that you don't have to carry past hurts within you. You can also use what you've learned to exercise forgiveness before it becomes a "past pain." In other words, you can make forgiveness a habit. To get that habit ingrained, each of you should write down at least three things you've learned while going through Steps One through Four. Then discuss these items. Together, identify five circumstances in which you'll use what you've learned in the future.

What you've learned is:

1.
2.
3.

What your child has learned is (optional):

1.
2.
3.

Congratulations! You've completed the exercises on forgiveness. Now you have the information and tools you need to forgive the hurts that are sure to occur from time to time. Remember, you can choose together how to deal with hurtful events. Do that, and you will have a closer, more loving relationship than ever before. Instead of hugging your hurts to yourself and suffering the destructive consequences, you can release those feelings to deepen your relationship and build trust and intimacy.

THE PLAN: DAYS 8–15

Parents and children often stumble and hurt each other without meaning to. Practicing forgiveness allows you to renew your relationship at any point. These exercises will help you discover how, with commitment, you can let go of past hurts and give your relationship a fresh start.

Step One: Know Your Expectations

You'll have a stronger starting place for renewal if you figure out what you're aiming for *before* you find yourself off the path. What do you expect from your relationship with your child at this stage? What would that dream relationship be like from this point on? Write a description of your dream relationship. Be as honest and specific as you can be. Use these questions as a starting place for your thoughts: What level of financial support are you expecting to give, and how will you manage it? Would your family (parents, siblings) or in-laws play a role, and if so, how so? Will you practice a religion, and if so, which one and how? What will you do for fun? What rituals will you want to do to deepen the ties? How will you express your love for one another?

After you have written this down, share it with your child. You've just taken the important step of describing and sharing the expectations each of you have for your relationship. Now you're ready to consider how you can deal with expectations in a way that strengthens your bond.

Step Two: Identify Disappointments

Sometimes expectations in parent-child love relationships go unfulfilled, leaving one or both individuals disappointed. Life may suddenly throw one or both of you off course with an illness or injury, the loss of a job, the death of someone close, or a natural disaster. You and your child may have difficulty because of different temperaments, leading to frustrations and cross-purposes. Or one or another of you may do something stupid or thoughtless or selfish. If and when you experience such disappointment, what will you do about it? Your reactions to disappointment, separately and together, will go a long way toward defining the future of your relationship.

In the space below, separately recall three occasions from your pasts when your expectations in an important (not necessarily parent-child) relationship were seriously disappointed. Describe each here, then explain how you responded. Did you walk out? Throw a tantrum? Verbally attack the other person? Sulk? Try to understand?

Your disappointments:

1. _____

_____

Your response _____

2. _____

_____

Your response _____

3. _____

_____

Your response _____

You've just taken an inventory of past disappointments and what you did about them. Now you can move forward to consider how your past reactions to disappointment may be affecting you in the present.

Step Three: Find Your Sore Spots

You've identified a few times when you didn't get what you expected from a relationship. The ways you reacted to disappointment had an effect on you, the other person, your relationship, and the situation. The effect may have been positive, destructive, or maybe a little of both. Look at the reactions each of you described above. On the scale below, rate each one for its relationship value, using the following scale:

1 = my reaction led to something greater in the situation
2 = on balance, my reaction helped the situation
3 = on balance, my reaction made the situation worse
4 = my reaction had a very destructive effect on the situation

For each reaction that you score 1 or 2, describe specifically why you believe it helped the situation and how. For each reaction you scored 3 or 4, suggest below a response that you believe would have had a more positive outcome. (Keep in mind that your reaction may have had an effect that looks more negative than it was. For example, your reaction may have brought the relationship to an end, but it needed to end.)

Your reactions to past relationships:

1. _____ 1   2   3   4
_____

2. _____ 1   2   3   4
_____

3. _____ 1   2   3   4
_____

This step gave each of you an opportunity to look at your past behavior and to assess whether it gave you the results you would want. Now take the next step to use that information and dig deeper.

Step Four: The Needs behind the Behavior

We all have expectations about our relationships. They help us define our needs and wants. Disappointments are just as inevitable, and if you learn from them, they can also provide great building material for your future with your child. As you recalled the incidents above and your reactions to them, you probably remembered many others. Those memories offer the opportunity to identify how you typically respond when your expectations are not met. The memories also contain clues to the unmet needs and insecurities behind your responses.

Describe your feelings at the time in terms of what you needed but did not receive. For example: a sense of security, predictability, respect, consideration, trust, support, tenderness, shared commitment, honesty, friendship, sense of importance, being heard, self-confidence, self-esteem, acceptance, safety, admiration, stability, kindness, faithfulness, space, loyalty.

For each disappointment, discuss and answer these questions:

1. When something went wrong, who did you blame?
2. When you reacted, did you have all the important information?
3. In hindsight, was your reaction the most helpful you could have made? If not, what would you substitute now? If yes, how can you learn from it?

This step has given you tools to develop a deeper level of understanding of what you need and hope for in relationships with your child. Now you can work to discover responses to disappointments that produce the results you want for a more loving relationship.

Step Five: Plan for Change and Renewal

Instead of letting disappointment and lack of forgiveness lead you down destructive paths again, you can make a plan to take a different, more constructive path. Look at your history as described above and create a hypothetical situation in which you feel disappointment in a relationship.

Hypothetical situation: _____

Based on what you've discussed so far, how would you want to deal with the disappointment together? Create a plan, including what you would need to enable yourself to:

1. Communicate the disappointment.

_____

_____

2. Ask for or offer forgiveness.

_____

_____

3. Put the disappointment behind you.

_____

_____

4. Discuss realistic expectations for the future.

_____

_____

5. Renew your commitment to take the next step in a loving relationship.

_____

_____

You've created a plan, in theory, that can help you get back on track when disappointments get in your way. This step-by-step approach can go a long way to moving the heat of your instinctive reactions to the back burner while you work together for renewal.

Step Six: Put It to Work

To make these exercises most useful, write down at least three things you've learned about dealing with disappointment while covering the first five steps. Then review the items you've written down. Commit yourself to using the skills you've learned over the next two weeks. You may or may not run into situations that seem directly related. That's okay. With the principles of these exercises in mind, keep track of situations in which you could have been disappointed, and which would have led to lack of forgiveness. At the end of two weeks, list what you have learned about putting your desire to forgive in action.

What you've learned is:

1.

2.

3.

Congratulations! You have completed the exercises on practicing forgiveness and renewing your relationships when you hit rough spots. With the information and tools you've been given, you can face future disappointments with the confidence to get through them and keep growing together. Rather than letting your raw feelings lead the way, you can work for renewal one step at a time.

THE POWER OF FORGIVENESS

Too many parent-child relationships suffer from a lack of loving bonds. Practicing forgiveness can build and heal those bonds. It starts with the parent modeling benevolence and generosity of spirit. Take the opportunity to teach your child the art of loving.

I have offered simple steps on the path toward forgiveness and all of its rewards. I realize that there are unforgivable acts. But to hold on to bitterness and hatred serves no good purpose. It only gives more power to the tormentor, and you certainly don't want to do that. It is natural to be angry and bitter, but the human spirit can soar above to heal and flourish. You cannot allow hostility and animosity to rule your life and destroy all your relationships. Discard emotional baggage and reach for the joy that forgiveness and compassion can provide you. I've given you the tools. You have the power to choose between a life of icy bitterness and isolation or one warmed by lasting, loving bonds.

11

Special Issue: Loving the Teen

This is a special chapter for those parents dealing with the strangest and most bizarre shift in their children's lives: adolescence. No set time frame is assigned. Read at your leisure as you experience the challenges—and also the joys—of having teens in the family.

It is said that parents who've raised teenagers go straight to heaven when they die because they have already seen hell. Teens have had a bad rap throughout history. They are often characterized as arrogant, self-centered, and shiftless burdens who sleep until noon and think only of the opposite sex and/or video games. Yet, long before the dawn of Nintendo and MTV, Socrates said: "Children today are tyrants. They contradict their parents. They gobble their food, and tyrannize their teachers."

Teens still strike fear into the hearts of many parents. While helping Dr. Phil with research for his book *Family First,* we conducted surveys on his Web site and collected more than 20,000 responses to our questions. One intriguing result regarding teens, which appeared to contradict perceived approaches to child-rearing, has tantalized my brain ever since. More than 90 percent of the mothers and fathers who responded said that they worry so much about the approaching teen years—often based on their own teenage experiences—that they guide their younger children with those years in mind, trying to prepare them for all of the worst-case scenarios like being pressured to have sex, drink alcohol, do drugs, or get involved in gang activities. Some parents also said they looked forward to the teen years because their children could start taking responsibility for themselves and be more helpful at home.

There are good things about the teen years. This is the time when young people begin to identify, pursue, and excel in their passions, which can make for a wonderful shared family experience. There is a special joy in seeing your children discover something that excites and inspires them. Parents often find themselves on a wild ride of highs and lows with their teens because of their excitability, mood swings, and emotional vulnerabilities. Most of these emotional swings are the result of major physiological and chemical changes they are undergoing as they hit puberty and move toward young adulthood. One thing is certain, life is rarely dull with a teen in the house.

TEEN TUMULT

Tina and her parents arrived at my office as a family in turmoil after going through the classic sixteen-year-old's nightmare. On her first trip on her first day as a licensed driver, Tina wrecked a new car, hitting a parked vehicle and then taking out part of her parents' garage for good measure.

Did I mention that she had the wreck because she got distracted while lighting a cigarette?

I barely had time to get through introductions before this family was locked in combat.

TINA'S FATHER, MIKE: "We just don't know what has happened to our baby girl. She's lost her judgment and doesn't seem to care about anything but her friends and her car. Now that is gone, due to her short attention span."

TINA: "Dad, you know I'm on the honor roll, and I'm a good driver. It was an accident. You had accidents before, and I didn't freak out because you ran into somebody's back bumper."

I called a time-out and attempted to steer the conversation in a more constructive direction. I asked what happened as a result of the accident.

TINA: "I was grounded, and I have never heard the end of it. Every time I want to do something, it is like going on trial. I want to become a foster child and move out of the house. I feel like I'm in prison."

MIKE: "Tina, it is just that we worry about you. We love you, but we know that you sometimes forget where you are. The accident is a good example."

TINA: "You don't understand, Dad. I am growing up, and I can make decisions. I am not your little girl anymore. I don't want to be at home all the time. So are we here to see if Dr. Lawlis can talk me into being happy with you? Is that it?"

I asked Tina if she would rather not have parents telling her what to do.

Tina collapsed into her chair sullenly. "Yeah, that's it. I am a prisoner."

It was Tina time.

I let her know that I understood her side of things. "It seems that life has taken a turn for the worse since you became a teenager, hasn't it?"

She nodded in agreement.

"In fact, you've felt misunderstood for a long time, and you are really unhappy, maybe even desperate?"

She nodded with tears in her eyes.

"Still, because of what is going on inside you, I imagine that you might be unhappy anywhere you live, don't you?"

She paused for several seconds, but finally nodded.

"I can see that you are stressed out, and it isn't just your parents. Every day at school you have to deal with the pressures of other kids pushing drugs, sex, and drinking—and on top of that is the fact that everyone says you've got to start thinking about your future and what you want to do about college and the rest of your life— even though you aren't really sure about anything right now, including who you are. Right?"

Tina's eyes glazed with tears.

"You're right," she said. "I didn't realize what it was, until you just said it. But I've got so much running through my brain. God, I am so tired all the time. What I really want to do is just sleep and let my brain rest. I am just stressed and tired all the time."

Her voice had the weary tone of someone who had just run a marathon. I could see that her parents were beginning to understand that Tina was dealing with more than they realized. She was also coming to the realization that her parents weren't the source of her problem. It was the internal turmoil more than anything else that was haunting her.

I told Tina that I could help her deal with the pressures and anxieties so that she could relax, get better rest, and feel more energetic and alert. She was grateful for that, and so were her parents. When a family is at war with itself, there are usually no winners. Problems don't get solved, because attacking and counterattacking become the focus. I had to put the brakes on so Tina and her parents could begin to listen to each other instead of attacking.

In our next three sessions, I taught this family how to relax and communicate more effectively. I used a device called the EmWave (Heartmath.com, 2006), a small gadget that has a computer in it to measure heart rate. It also sets a calmer rate of breathing. Whenever one of them began to stress, a buzzer went off. We stopped then and did relaxation exercises.

It worked very well. Each family member quickly learned to remain calm to keep the buzzers silent, allowing us to discuss the situation without emotional flare-ups. Tina felt comfortable talking about her feelings without flashing at her parents and making them defensive. Even better, her parents were able to show their love and concern without being interrupted by the teen's accusations or defiance. It took three sessions, but they were able to work things out. It was rewarding to see Tina communicate with her parents in a more mature manner, and even more rewarding to see the family's bonds restored and even strengthened.

Your Teen's State of Mind: An Assessment

The teen years bring challenges and stresses that test the strongest, most loving family relationships. Some parent-child relationships cannot handle the stress. Parents who insist on treating their teens as children often have the most difficult time. I know many adults in their fifties who still become children around their parents because their relationship has never matured beyond preadolescence. This is not love; it is role-playing to avoid conflict and uncomfortable realities. Both the teens and the parents need to make adjustments to keep the family bonds strong. Teens often have difficulty articulating their needs and emotions, so they need help analyzing their feelings. Parents need to reach out even when they feel they are being pushed away. When they don't adjust, I've seen long-term damage result. It is not unusual for parents and their children to become alienated and to stop communicating because of things that occurred during the teenage years.

A greater danger is teen suicide. Studies have identified three primary factors that predict a teen's likelihood of attempting suicide; poor family relationships, isolation from peers, and a history of physical abuse. Strong and supportive family bonds—and peer friendships too—are incredibly important for a teen's mental health and mature development. In my own teen years, I leaned on my mother and her loving pep talks, in which she would assure me of my family's love, support, and faith in me. She told me that I was destined to do important things and that I had to stick to my values and beliefs.

Parents need to understand that teens are often highly emotional, not because they are bad kids or hyperactive but because their hormones are in an uproar. As they enter puberty, hormones cascade into the system, hindering their judgment and their planning abilities. It helps to know what is typical behavior for teens and what may be a sign of potential trouble. Here is a brief assessment chart for teen behavior.

For the items described below, decide whether your teenager is behaving in these ways all the time (A), some of the time (S), rarely (R), or never (N).

1. My teen is obsessed with political, religious, or ecological issues.

   A   S   R   N

2. My teen's personal grooming is poor.

   A   S   R   N

3. My teen complains about life and the world in general.

   A   S   R   N

4. My teen lacks social skills and seems isolated from peers.

   A   S   R   N

5. My teen offers unrealistic views of the world.

   A   S   R   N

6. My teen is dangerously overconfident.

   A   S   R   N

7. My teen thinks all adults are stupid.

   A   S   R   N

8. My teen's interest in hobbies and goals has disappeared.

   A   S   R   N

9. My teen shows interest in a broad range of subjects and goals.

   A   S   R   N

10. My teen demands privacy and time alone.

    A   S   R   N

11. My teen constantly needs to be with friends.

    A   S   R   N

12. My teen expresses anger toward the "in crowd."

    A   S   R   N

13. My teen comes home past curfew.

    A   S   R   N

14. My teen demands money without explanation.

    A   S   R   N

15. My teen's mood swings depending on whether or not I give in to demands.

    A   S   R   N

16. My teen prefers gang activities to school.

    A   S   R   N

17. My teen talks about material goods like clothes and cars.

    A   S   R   N

18. My teen talks about drugs and drug paraphernalia.

    A   S   R   N

19. My teen swaps or matches clothing with friends.

    A   S   R   N

20. My teen lives in an abusive relationship.

    A   S   R   N

Scoring

This test is actually two tests in one. The odd-numbered items (1, 3, 5, 7, 9, 11, 13, 15, 17, 19) describe typical behavior in the development of an adolescent. *The higher the number on these items, the higher the level of intensity in the process of this age. This may reflect on the challenges in the relationship, but is NOT a danger signal.* The even-numbered items (2, 4, 6, 8, 10, 12, 14, 16, 18, 20) describe the danger signs that require immediate attention to the relationship.

For each item, give 4 points for each A answer, 2 points for each S, and 1 point for each R answer. For the Typical Teen score, add the odd-numbered items for a sum in the range from 0 to 40. For the Teen in Danger score, add the even-numbered items for a sum in the range from 0 to 40. Compare your results below:

Typical Teen Scoring Interpretation

0–10   Teen has not developed fully. Many teens do not have a major change.

11–25   Mild changes, but appropriate for this stage. It would be good to have weekly talks about issues.

26–40   This range indicates your teen is undergoing major changes, and you might need help too, as you might be a poor role model. Your family should seek professional counseling.

Teen in Danger Scoring Interpretation

0–10   Although your teen may be showing only a few signs of problems, you need to make a priority of communicating. Supportive daily talks are required. The time to act is now.

11–25   It is time to bring in some experts. Set up family counseling for insights and direction. Show your love for your teen by listening and spending time together. DO NOT LET THIS GROW OR DELAY. Do not procrastinate or blame anyone.

26–40   This score indicates a serious problem, and you might need some help yourself. You might be unconsciously modeling a relationship issue or some anger that feeds apathy. You and your teen need attention. The whole family should get involved.

THE NEUROLOGY OF TEEN TURMOIL

Adolescence is the transition period between childhood and adulthood. Hundreds of years ago, teenagers were considered adults and given all of those responsibilities and privileges, including work, marriage, child-rearing, military duty, and ruling power. Yet earlier cultures provided more "rites of passage" that recognized the transitional stage. Young males served apprenticeships in the trades and crafts. Young females were presented as debutantes and candidates for marriage and motherhood.

That recognized period of transition and maturation has been largely lost in the United States and Europe, as young people stay in school for longer periods and avoid the responsibilities of adulthood, delaying their social maturation. Instead of taking their places as contributing members of society as soon as they hit their teens, they now have a more extended adolescence.

This has caused several problems for society. The sex drive emerges, even though young people no longer get married in adolescence, as they did in past cultures. Higher levels of testosterone in males also trigger aggressive tendencies that are now met by sports competition—or gang activity—rather than the combat, raids, and hunting parties of the past.

As they enter the teenage years, young people undergo physiological changes that make them vulnerable to the sort of accident that Tina experienced. Because of hormonal and chemical changes as their brains literally rewire themselves, teens are easily distracted. They often have difficulty multitasking. On top of that, there is the volatile blend of inflated levels of self-confidence and poor risk-assessment capability. Imagine Tina, a first-time driver, who has just passed her driving test with flying colors. Her confidence level is soaring, even though she has little on-the-road experience. She gets behind the wheel, flush with excitement at this newfound freedom. She tries to light a cigarette, perhaps to calm herself, while driving (poor risk assessment) and talking with friends (multitasking challenge). Her overconfidence meets with her lack of experience meets with her poor risk judgment and inability to multitask: scratch one new car, a parked car, and the side of the garage.

Enter the ticked-off parents.

But parents need to understand that teens face unique challenges. Up to this stage, the human brain is growing, creating hundreds of thousands of neurons that allow children to absorb information and learn at the fastest rates of their lives. Ninety percent of what a person learns occurs in the first eight years of school, when the brain is capable of rapidly creating huge libraries of information and memories. That is the reason learning to speak a different language or to play a musical instrument is easier to accomplish when we are younger.

Think of the brain as a big tree, spreading out its branches to catch the sun. At this age, every day a new leaf is formed. That is why child prodigies are plentiful. The amazing learning capabilities of young people give their parents cause to hope for great achievements and future opportunities. Then the teen years hit—and sometimes it seems like the brain goes into hibernation. There are scientific reasons for this. On the eve of adolescence, the brain stops growing and instead begins pruning back those branches of neurons. Thousands of them are trimmed as the brain's "wiring" is reorganized, effectively "specializing" according to those areas that appear to have the greatest potential for survival.

During this rewiring process, teens can appear to be "in a fog," or even comatose. Parents get frustrated if they don't understand this, and even when they do. A friend of mine said his wife, aware of what happens to teen brains, took to commanding her distracted teen son, "Engage frontal lobes!" when he had trouble focusing on tasks.

Think of teen brains as computers that are slow to perform functions because so many processes are taking place at once. Brain scans verify that that is essentially what is going on. The primary slowdown occurs in the prefrontal lobe, the area right above your eyes, which is like the brain's command center. It tells the rest of the brain how to perform tasks and also serves as a problem-solving center that plays a critical role in the execution of cognitive tasks.

When young people reach maturity, at about age twenty-six, their brains are more efficient. But teen brains do not operate at maximum efficiency. They have to work harder to focus and think through complex issues. Adult brains can distribute the load more easily, according to studies by Dr. Susan F. Tapert, associate professor of psychiatry at the University of California.

Slower brain functions make teens vulnerable to stress. They may be able to function at high levels in some activities, such as driving a car or dealing with a class assignment, but when stress is added to the equation, things can go south quickly. This alone may explain why teens are susceptible to thoughtless and impulsive behavior. Their overtaxed cortexes have difficulty making judgments and thinking ahead, so teens tend to respond more to external factors like peer pressure. They also are likely to act without thinking things through.

IMPLICATIONS OF BRAIN FUNCTION STUDIES

The brain studies help explain a great deal about teenage behavior that otherwise might mystify parents. There are societal implications as well. For example, adolescents traditionally have made better soldiers than mature adults because action-oriented teens don't reason out the travesties of war. They are more likely to sacrifice their lives without resistance. The age-old dramas of teen romance, such as the classic, *Romeo and Juliet,* are due to the fiery passions of youth coupled with their inability to comprehend future consequences. The same behavioral characteristics explain why so many young people get involved in gangs and drugs and other dangerous activities. They lack the ability to foresee what lies ahead on those paths.

Tragically, teens are both vulnerable to the temptations of recreational and addictive drugs and likely to suffer the most grievous long-term effects. Marijuana and cocaine are especially vicious in creating disabilities. During this vulnerable time, when the brain is rewiring for adulthood, these drugs can interfere with nerve growth and halt the process, affecting memory and long-term brain capacity. I believe that our brains have the power to heal themselves over time, and I feel that nearly any brain problem can be overcome with correct treatment. But damage caused by teenage drug use presents substantial challenges.

HOW TO LOVE YOUR TEEN

A great deal has been learned about teen brain capacities, and much of their behavior can be explained by changes taking place in their bodies. But parents have to put that knowledge to use in relating to their teens. A little understanding goes a long way during this vulnerable period. Parents who make the effort have the opportunity to create strong and loving bonds that will reap a lifetime of rewards.

The principles for loving your teen are set on two relationship levels: the unconscious (neurological) and the conscious (psychological). I promise that if parents follow my guidance, they will make it through their children's teen years without significant scars, and maybe even with some wonderful experiences and memories.

First of all, I need to advise you of a few major don'ts for dealing with a teenager. I have dealt with thousands of teens and their parents. You can spare your family a great deal of grief—and months, if not years, of friction—by heeding my warnings.

- Don't overreact, scream, or moralize. This only fuels the flames.
- Don't excuse or condone the use of drugs or chemicals. They do unimaginable damage, and can even paralyze the brain.
- Don't blame yourself or let your child blame you. This is not a blame game. It is about personal responsibility.
- Don't strike deals, or bribe your teen to stop dangerous behavior. Develop good negotiation skills.
- Don't accept the excuse that "they all do it." This is a sign of weakness and a lack of self-control.
- Don't make threats you don't intend to carry out. You lose every time.

Those are preventive measures. Now, let's look at some pro-active methods and tools for strengthening your loving bonds with teens. These are proven. I know they work if properly implemented. I also recommend that you create a relaxed environment for putting them into play. My father and I used to enjoy shooting rifles at tin cans. Afterward, we would put the guns down (highly recommended) and talk about our concerns. I have fond memories of those times because I felt I had my father's full attention. I knew he cared, and that he was listening to me.

SENSORY TOOLS

Although your teen may be as tall as you are, the sensory tools offered in the earlier chapters for dealing with children will still be effective. The teen brain pays more attention to external cues than internal ones, making it highly receptive to sensory inputs.

Seeing

Teens react strongly to visual stimulus. Take advantage of that by looking your teen in the eye when you want to get a message across. Use graphic illustrations, including drawings and schematics, to support your words. When I worked with teen patients in New York, I had a chalkboard next to my desk. I drew out action plans the same way a coach marks out plays, with X's and O's. The teens responded eagerly, making their own charts. This method helps them think through possible outcomes and risk factors at a time when their brains have difficulty with those tasks.

Using the timeline, have the teen specify what actions he is taking or will be taking. He may be thinking of rebelling against the school or against you in some way, or putting off homework. Then

Timeline Demonstration

back up to yesterday (or any remote significant time in which some event seemed to promote this action). Examples are arguments that created a mind-set, unfair events, remarks made, or even actions remote from immediate impact, such as the Twin Towers disaster in New York or an inspirational speech given over the television.

The history step is an interesting one, because it gives some context for thinking things through. The projected future step offers intriguing insight into young minds. Whatever the future projection, the teen should always consider other options. *What if your daughter's boyfriend sees her flirting with his best friends and walks away from their relationship?* Teens' brains function in very linear patterns, so they often have difficulty thinking through a full range of possibilities and potential outcomes. *What if your son gets caught skipping school and his friends turn on him?*

A word of caution: Adolescents are not good at planning ahead, which is why you may find them struggling with the concept of college and career. Ninety percent of the time they will report only glamourous TV professions as their unrealistic goals. They simply can't get their overheated brains to wrap around future concepts. That is why they often take risks, seek thrills, and go for short-term rewards over long-term benefits. They are short-sighted because their brains are effectively short-circuited. Some have said this explains why teen girls often go for the "bad boys" over the nice guys.

Visual imagery is a very powerful tool for teens, too. One of the most effective things I've done to reach and help teen drug abusers is to have them visualize their lives ahead by one year and then five years and, finally, in their final years. I've also used visualization as a tool for teens to help them find ways out of difficult situations. Lucy was a sweet girl who had trouble saying no when her peers offered her alcohol. I walked her through a number of scenarios in which she used my suggested methods for turning down drinks without seeming "uncool." By going through this process, she figured out comfortable ways to hang on to her friends and social standing while staying clear of alcohol.

Hearing

The second most powerful stimulant for the typical teen brain is sound. This will come as no surprise to parents who've had their eardrums ache after getting into a teen's car. Again, there are biological reasons for this seemingly insane teen tendency. The adolescent brain craves the booming bass sounds because those frequencies stimulate specific areas of the brain that are slowed by the rewiring process. Other frequencies soothe their overtaxed brains. Certain strong, rhythmic beats play into the teen's need for exterior stimulation. It is not accidental that armies and football teams are sent into battle by music featuring rapid drumbeats and rhythmic pulsations.

Parents can use their teenager's sensitivity to music as a tool. If you want to have a talk with your teen, put on music that your teen enjoys but that also creates the mood or environment most conducive to your discussion. There is proper music for every occasion, after all, from church services to sports bars. When my grandfather wanted me to settle down and have a serious talk, he would first have me sing, "Just a Closer Walk with Thee" or "Home on the Range." I'm no Willie Nelson, but my grandfather must have appreciated the calming effect that music had on me, if not the quality of my voice.

In my therapeutic work with teens and their parents, I've had great success with another form of music, the drums. Research has found that drumming cadences drive brain frequencies. When two drummers play together, matching rhythms, their minds and bodies fall into synch. Some studies on therapeutic drumming have put warring gang members together with drums. At first, they play warring beats, and the sound is every bit as chaotic as their street fights. But after ten to twenty minutes of continuous drumming, their drumming becomes synchronized and rhythmic. After several drumming sessions, even longtime enemies can begin to form bonds, these studies have found.

I've had similar results using drum therapy with teens and their parents. It works so well, I've used it in my own family. My grandson was having difficulties in school after the death of his father. The next summer, he visited me. We played drums and guitar together, even composed a few songs. My grandson found some peace in the music we made. After he returned home, his mother noted a significant increase in his self-esteem. I'm happy to say he is now a classical guitarist, and doing very well.

Healing Touch

Your surly teen may not seem like he needs a hug, but adolescents are extremely responsive to a healing touch. Their young bodies are finely tuned and highly responsive. I've learned to accurately detect the level of stress a teen is feeling simply by shaking hands. If the teen's hand is moist with sweat or cold, it is a good bet that the kid is anxious. If the arm is rigid and moves robotically when I shake hands, the teen is likely to be resistant, angry, and prone to flight.

My mother was a junior high counselor, and she had a sixth sense for relating to kids. I watched her connect with many teens. One of her favorite methods was to shake hands with kids who were acting out and then hold on to their hands until they had resolved the problem. She didn't use a death grip. But she was able to communicate through her touch that she cared and was committed to helping. My mother knew, either from her studies, experience, or intuition, that teens can be helped to focus through touch. In my own teaching days, I reined in problem kids by shaking hands with them and then holding on to their hands as I guided them into my office. I maintained my hold while talking to them. If a student tried to withdraw his hand, I explained that I was checking his pulse rate or that I wanted to hold on so he knew I was there for him. I generally got very good results.

LISTEN AND LEARN

In a report entitled *When Did We Start Drugging Teens and Stop Listening to Them?* I found that 52 percent of adolescents who saw therapists in 2002 were given prescriptions for antidepressants, while nearly 10 percent less were given counseling. These statistics bother me because they reflect a tendency to prescribe pills for teens rather than listening to them and helping them resolve their issues. It also troubles me that the number of children diagnosed with ADHD has reached an all-time high, even as research has shown that 65 percent of such diagnoses are incorrect.

We need to do more listening and less labeling. And I'm not talking about spending "quality time," or simply listening when there is a problem to be discussed. If you can't talk to each other when there is no crisis, how can you talk when there is one? Parents need to spend time with their children, simply talking about things that don't matter, so that the lines of communication are open for those things that really *do* matter. It is an investment that pays incredible dividends.

So listen to their favorite singers, talk with them about friends and school, and learn their tastes in clothing, cars, movies, and television shows. If you don't know your teen's favorite teacher, favorite fast food, or favorite television show, you are not tuned in. So don't be surprised if your teen tunes you out.

Show empathy, interest, and understanding of your teen's world. Believe it or not, she might be interested in hearing about your own likes and dislikes and experiences in junior high and high school. You danced? You got into trouble? You experienced peer pressure? You weren't always the perfect role model? Open yourself up for questioning and be honest. Share your values, and the experiences and lessons that helped you choose them.

BE SUPPORTIVE AND ACCEPTING

Parents may feel like scenery in a teen's life sometimes, but the fact is, your support and acceptance are critical to your child's success. Studies have shown that the most significant predictors of a teen's susceptibility to both suicide and criminal activity are the levels of parental support at home. The more words spoken in a day correlated with less trouble. Your child needs to know that you care. And teens need to hear it, see it, feel it, more often than most because of all the insecurities that plague them day in and day out. This does not mean you should strive to be their best friend, give freedoms that they can't handle, or allow them to think that they can do no wrong. You don't do them any favors that way.

But you do yourself and your teen a tremendous service when you demonstrate to them by listening, touching, accepting, supporting, and guiding them with your loving attention. Acceptance is important to everyone, but it is especially critical for teens, because they desperately want to understand where they fit in. They may not let on, but they are scared about what awaits them when they go off to college or the working world. They need to know that they will be accepted. And if you don't show your acceptance of them as teens, there are throngs of street gangs, drug dealers, abusers, and manipulators just waiting for eager young prey to walk out of your house and into their hands. I can't stress enough how important it is that you give your teen encouragement.

My father was a pilot, and he would take me flying as a treat. Naturally I grew up wanting to get a pilot's license. He gave me my first lesson at fifteen. Afterward, I was eager for encouragement. I asked him how I did.

His response was, "You don't want me to brag on you, do you?"

Of course I wanted his praise—and that may have been his way of giving it—but it left me feeling like I'd failed my first test at being a man like him. It was a small exchange, but it stuck with me even after I got my license and became a pilot. My father didn't give me what I was looking for, and that lack of encouragement hurt. Make sure you give your teen at least a small dose of it at every opportunity.

All kids go through hard times. They don't always talk about it. So it is important to let your teen know that you appreciate her, and that you understand that she is dealing with stresses and pressures outside the home. There was a new CEO whose first announcement to his board of directors was that the company was not making enough mistakes. His philosophy was that only by making mistakes can you learn to create success. He proved to be a very successful leader because his employees were not afraid of making mistakes. I think parents should use that same philosophy in raising their children. You can't assume you know all the answers (after all, the joke says that having teens lowers a parent's IQ by fifty points). But I think the greatest thing you can do as the parent of a teen is to give her the support and the love she needs to go out in the world and make her own mistakes without fear.

CHAOS THEORY

Adolescence is a chaotic experience. The mind, body, and emotions are all over the place. Turmoil and passion rule. We remember our teen years as painful and exhilarating. Some speculate that adolescence is an evolutionary bridge in which human reasoning was compromised so that there could be cross-fertilization between tribes to allow for genetic advances. The whole Romeo and Juliet, Sharks and Jets thing takes on a different light in that framework. Maybe that's why the ancient Greeks considered this stage of life a cosmic joke for their enjoyment.

I just wish so many families didn't have to struggle through this period in their children's lives. There are many joys to having teens in the house. Chaos also creates opportunity. The teen years are a period of rebirth, and they give parents the opportunity to strengthen bonds with their children. I urge parents to leap on that opportunity; bonds that are strengthened in the teen years will likely grow stronger for decades to come.

Your teens will make mistakes and misjudgments. Count on it. Know it is coming. Guide them. Love them. Listen to them. Support them. Forgive them. And encourage them.

Soon, your teen will be your adult child. Before you know it, the teen years will be a memory. It is up to you to influence how those memories are perceived. Listen now. Support. Encourage. Forgive. Nurture. And bask in the rewards for years to come.

12

The Spirit of Love

This is the tenth and final segment in the 90-day program. Religious preferences are matters of personal choice, but most children have questions about the spiritual elements of life on earth and beyond. This chapter offers assistance in providing answers and a spiritual foundation for your child. You are allotted five days for this concluding segment, but be aware that for many people, the quest for answers and fulfillment in this realm is a life's journey.

Religion is our attempt to explain the divine, spiritual aspects of our existence. Many religions define the powerful spiritual force as "love." Most of us are introduced to love as the bond between parents and child before we understand it in a religious context.

Psychologists rarely talk about spirituality and its effects on behavior, for two basic reasons. Most have no training in that arena, and our experience teaches us that religion is often the source of guilt-related psychological turmoil. It might also be that many psychologists are uncomfortable acknowledging that there could be other forces acting on a child besides the academically accepted influences of human physiology, behavioral science, and environmental factors. It is also true that scientific training holds that only measurable dimensions can be studied, which leaves out the most inspirational dynamic in human consciousness—the answer to the question, *Why do I exist?*

This question is the central challenge to both theology and science, and religion approaches the challenge in very different ways. I respect both camps, but I embrace anything that can be a positive influence for a child. And children very often have questions about existence. If I haven't heard them all, I've certainly heard a lot of them: *Who made me? Why am I here? What happens when I die? Do I live as a ghost? Does it really matter if I am "good" while I am alive? Who decides whether I go to heaven or hell?*

Most children have similar questions, even if they don't express them. Once they grasp that their parents are fallible human beings who need love and support, kids figure there must be some superior being overseeing us all. *Someone has to make the rules, right? Who decides what is right and wrong?*

Children need to know they are special and that there is a reason for their existence. Otherwise, they have no grounding for any other reality than the one imposed upon them by circumstances. In my experience, most children sense that they are part of something greater than themselves. I believe they need to be assured of that. It grounds them and validates them. Young people have a great need to feel that they belong, that they fit in, and that they are loved.

SPIRITUAL BEINGS

Joseph came to our clinic with a fascinating history and a very mature attitude for a boy just seven years old. He'd been adopted at the age of two from a Russian orphanage. His adoptive mother was told that when doctors delivered him, they'd thought he was still-born because he was so underweight. He apparently was discovered alive in a room where they'd placed what they thought was his dead body.

Still, his birth mother had given him up, and after two months in virtual isolation, unloved and untouched, he was transferred to the orphanage. He was adopted two years later by an American couple with two other adopted children who were sisters from Mexico, four and two years older.

The adoptive parents were kind and gentle people, and they had bonded easily with their two adopted girls. Joseph proved to be much more of a challenge. In fact, after six months they decided the Russian toddler was not a good fit for their family, but their attempts to have him placed elsewhere failed.

They came to me for help with Joseph because they felt unqualified to deal with his problems. The boy did not respond to them emotionally. He understood what he was told and complied with instructions, but he was distant and unresponsive emotionally. You had the sense that he was "in another world," and only vaguely interested in the people or things around him.

We put Joseph through a series of intelligence tests and brain scans. They revealed no serious problems. He performed reasonably well on the intelligence tests. There were some detectable problems with levels of concentration, but we could not see any evidence of ADHD patterns. However, there were indicators of anxiety and depression. I was surprised during my first interview with him, because he seemed more mature than most kids his age. He had the "old soul" quality. It was a little strange because he also had the steady gaze and deeper voice of a much older kid. And this seven-year-old had a keen awareness of what was going on.

His first words were, "Do you think I can stay with this family?"

Since he talked like a much older young person, I addressed him in a similar manner. I told him that it wasn't that his adoptive parents wanted to get rid of him. They just felt they needed to understand him better.

Again, Joseph met my gaze calmly, and with a very mature voice asked: "Do you understand me? I seem to be so different from anyone else."

I tried to assure him, "You are different, and you are special."

He stared at me for a long time, as if taking my measure. Finally, he said: "Did you see them? Do you know they are here?"

I was afraid he might be having psychotic episodes.

"Who is here? Who do you think you see?" I asked.

"The angels who have been with me; they talk to me about what I am supposed to do. They say I am special."

Concerned, I inquired as to whether these "angels" were negative or positive influences on the boy. "Do these angels tell you bad things to do, or to harm anyone or even hurt yourself?"

"No, they just want me to know I am a special child with a mission on earth. They've come to me as far back as I remember. They have been the only people who tell me they love me and they look after me."

With my encouragement, Joseph elaborated, describing the angels as spiritual guides whom he believed had cared for him at birth and protected him when he was briefly given up for dead and then when he was placed in an orphanage.

It didn't matter whether I believed Joseph's story or not; what mattered at that point was that he believed in the existence of these spiritual beings, which had enabled him to survive the challenges of his early days on earth. We spent more than an hour talking about his communication with his angels and how they influenced his life. I had him draw pictures of them. He also drew symbols that the angels had shown him, including a circle with a fiery red stone in the middle and a triangle with a shiny star at the top.

Joseph appeared to have a strong spiritual nature, and I was careful not to question the authenticity of his benevolent and protective angels. From a psychologist's perspective, I would interpret these angels as a defense mechanism created by the boy's subconscious—a positive development that shows he is capable of finding comfort and assurances within himself. From a purely personal perspective, I keep an open mind about such things. I'm willing to believe that perhaps some spiritual guidance was delivered to this child to help him. I am comfortable with either conclusion. My definition of personal power is what we believe and trust.

And so I encouraged Joseph to stay in communication with his angels and to seek their guidance. I told him to work at trusting and fitting in with his adoptive family, and to listen to his teachers. He was excited by that prospect, and he responded well. A year later, he was much more involved with his adoptive family and getting good grades in school. The parents were extremely happy because, for the first time, loving bonds had formed. Were these real angels? What do you think?

Spiritual Grounding

Children are often tuned in to spiritual things much more than their parents might suspect because kids can't always express complex ideas and their feelings about them. To help you tune in to your child's level of spirituality, I've devised the following assessment test.

Please note for each entry the rate of frequency that applies: always (A), often (O), sometimes (S), or never (N).

1. My child talks about spiritual concepts and their effects.

   A   O   S   N

2. My child feels there is a reason for existing.

   A   O   S   N

3. My child is comfortable when death is mentioned.

   A   O   S   N

4. My child is optimistic that anything may happen.

   A   O   S   N

5. My child appears to have faith in justice being served.

    A   O   S   N

6. Our family talks about religious beliefs.

    A   O   S   N

7. My child has a personal relationship with a divine figure.

    A   O   S   N

8. My child communicates with a divine figure or force.

    A   O   S   N

9. My child hears stories of spiritual or moral value.

    A   O   S   N

10. Our family observes religious or spiritual practices.

    A   O   S   N

11. My child is taught religious or spiritual philosophy.

    A   O   S   N

12. If I have a blended family of mixed religious or spiritual philosophies, both are discussed, and resolutions are found.

    A   O   S   N

13. My child uses a moral foundation for judging right from wrong.

    A   O   S   N

14. My child talks about spiritual concepts, such as an afterlife.

    A   O   S   N

15. My child has questions about immortality and the soul.

    A   O   S   N

Scoring

Count every Always (A) as a 4, every Often (O) as a 3, every Sometimes (S) as a 2, and every Never (N) as a 1. Add up the fifteen items for a score in the range of 15 to 60 and compare your score to the following ranges:

50–60   You and your child pay strong attention to spiritual concepts.

38–49   You and your child have good awareness of spiritual and religious concepts, but you need to stay tuned in.

25–37   You and your child should communicate more about spiritual beliefs.

15–24   Your child is in need of more spiritual training and background.

A note of caution: This assessment may be overgeneralized when applied to different age groups. Interest in and understanding of spiritual matters varies widely depending on age and maturity levels. The following chart offers a basic outline of spiritual development in children.

Up to the age of two years, children have little grasp of complex spiritual matters. Their understanding of the world is mostly limited to their parents and other family members who provide nurturing and meet other basic needs. This is the time in which trust is learned, and children may harbor fears of abandonment. Special consideration should be made by the parents to ensure that these psychological and spiritual needs for security are met. Otherwise, a child's spiritual development may be severely disrupted.

Spiritual Development

Developmental Age	Spiritual Task	View of Supreme Being	Seeds	Spiritual Baggage
0–2 years	Learning to trust; concept of love from another	Parent	Hope, trust, courage, and love	Mistrust, abandonment, deprivation, inconsistency
3–7 years	Empathy and actions of love; interpersonal respect beyond physical	Super-parent, Santa Claus, source of good	Imagination, courage, loyalty	Shame/doubt, guilt, fears
6–12 years	Appreciating differences in others; discovering religious principles	Teacher or judge	Will, purpose	Perfectionism, literalness, self-abasement
Teens and Adults	Finding one's place/role in Supreme Being's world	Idealized symbol	Faithfulness, personal myth/story	Group authority compromising autonomy

In the next phase (3–7 years), the child begins to perceive other parental figures as godlike. Santa Claus, who knows if children are "naughty or nice," is but one of the cultural icons they embrace. Children of this age want to feel worthy of love, so they tend to have warm feelings for Santa, the Easter Bunny, Big Bird, Barney, and other parental or guardian figures.

The next stage is less warm and fuzzy. The preteen is much more suspicious and apprehensive of all things, including those that are spiritual. These kids are very sensitive to finding a place in life, and they usually seek perfection. They want perfect parents, perfect teachers, and a perfect world. Their childhood fantasies are still important to them. Since they know they are not perfect, they are anxious about dealing with any symbol that might bring flaws.

Individuals are more accepting of imperfection as they grow older. Their spiritual lives often dim as they become more aware of darker realities. They tend to be drawn to high-risk activities, menacing characters, and the cultural fringe. Drugs, alcohol, gangs, cults, and sexual experimentation can seem very appealing at this stage, much to a parent's dismay.

REACHING FOR THE "RIGHT" SPIRITUALITY

We are a world of many religions and faiths, offering spiritual guidance, meditation on life's meaning, and the ultimate sources of wisdom and power. As the saying goes, "God is known by a thousand names." Human beings have searched for spiritual answers and the mysteries of life after death since the earliest civilizations. Whether the spiritual "voice" comes from within ourselves or beyond our vision, most people acknowledge that there may be a higher level of existence beyond the common human experience.

Over the generations and across civilizations, humans have looked to nature in the stars, the sun, the moon, water, and other elements as spiritual sources or symbols. Others have focused on all-knowing, all-powerful deities who have either passed through lives on earth or always existed at a level beyond. Some see these entities as entirely benevolent, while others believe their spiritual guides have punitive qualities.

To be sure, evil men and women have manipulated spiritual

beliefs to destructive and horrifying purposes. The Salem witch tri-als and the Holocaust are just two examples. I have observed abuse from religious cults that espouse religious values but manipulate and prey upon their followers. On the *Dr. Phil* show, children have told of being manipulated and controlled by spiritual leaders who wielded threats that they would "burn in hell forever" if they did not comply.

At some point in our lives, and often throughout our lives, most of us seek spiritual connections that go beyond our relationships with other humans. Often, the spiritual divine is defined as *love*. The loving bonds formed between humans may well be a survival instinct, but our quest for a connection to a higher level of existence that is often a model of selflessness is not so easily rationalized—just as rational thinking (science) has so far been unable to fully explain the existence of the universe.

SPIRITUALITY AND LOVE

No one yet has figured out how the universe was created, but many still strive to know its secrets. We may be unable to comprehend all dimensions of life with the limits of our sensory systems and limited brains. We know, for example, that our vision is limited to a narrow span of light frequencies and colors. Birds and cats can see more than we do. Bats can hear a broader range of frequencies, and dogs can detect scents much better than their "masters."

While we generally acknowledge the existence of some levels of intuition, and even "extrasensory perception," we have yet to come up with a way to measure or exploit the suspected "sixth sense." Sixty percent of the population believes in ghosts or apparitions of dead people, yet no one has ever measured that energy or fully explained it. Then again, no one has ever seen an atom, which sci-ence accepts as nature's primary building block.

When we have no rational explanation, visual confirmation, or way to measure something we believe to exist, we take it "on faith." This is particularly true in spiritual matters. Children often seek explanations and confirmation of the existence of spiritual beings. It seems to be a basic human need for most of us. Children, and perhaps most humans, at some point seek confirmation of these spiritual concepts:

1. Everyone is connected.
2. Justice is ultimately served, and forgiveness is a strength.
3. Each individual has a higher purpose.
4. There is a source of infinite wisdom.
5. Love conquers all, even death.

EVERYONE IS CONNECTED

The first spiritual concept that children seem to grasp is that there are bonds that link all humans. They reach out to strangers, just as adults feel compassion for people on the other side of the world. It is this deep empathy that unites us. This is the reason we can understand the feelings of another person even when we don't share the same language or culture. When we can't connect, for whatever reason, distrust and fear fill the gap, and often hostilities and confrontation result.

In the Cold War, we felt threatened by the Soviet Union and maintained constant vigilance in fear of a nuclear attack. The Soviets were portrayed as evil, angry people, and we were afraid for our lives. A group of missionaries from my boyhood church visited Russia. When they returned, one of their group, a woman, told our congregation, "The mothers love their babies just like we love ours." Her message was that despite the differences of our governments, we were linked by our humanity. The Russians loved, feared, and struggled just as we did. For a small-town boy in west Texas, this was a powerful notion, and it dramatically altered my perception of our Cold War enemy.

That is a hopeful notion, because what we have in common offers us common ground, a place for resolving differences and, perhaps, coming together in peace. Children who sense or understand that can be reached by parents who help them get to that common ground through empathy. The power of human empathy is most evident in those incidents of selfless acts, when men and women sacrifice their own safety, endangering their health and even their lives to help strangers. No wonder children, and adults too, are enthralled and touched by "heroic" acts, such as that of the New Yorker who leapt onto the subway tracks to save another man while his children watched, or the soldiers, firemen, police officers, and others who perform similar feats. These highly empathetic, selfless acts of sacrifice, which form the basis of so many of our myths, our legends, and our religions too, offer lessons and opportunities for bonding with your child on a spiritual level.

Activities for Life Connections
1. Talk with your child about feelings we all share.
2. Discuss the challenges faced by people around the world and how they must feel fear and hopelessness.
3. Share stories of selfless and heroic acts and what they say about our shared humanity and the spiritual nature of life.

JUSTICE AND FORGIVENESS

We see injustices go unanswered every day, whether in the form of brutal cruelty, economic disparity, or simply those with power abusing those without it. Children see it on their own level at day care, in school, on the playground or bus, and, sadly, at home too. They see prejudice and bullying and preferential treatment, and they feel outrage and despair over it, whether it is based on skin color, socioeconomic background, athletic ability, attractiveness, or academic standing.

All of us learn eventually that life is not always fair, justice is not always delivered, and, as the motto of the confirmed cynic goes, "No good deed goes unpunished." Our hunger for justice is one of the appeals of spirituality and the promises of heaven, hell, karma, judgment day, reincarnation, and other basic concepts of the after-life. The general promise is that one day, justice will prevail; the good will be rewarded, and the bad punished. The hope of many people of faith and deep spirituality is that they will be rewarded, sooner or later, for living unselfish, moral, caring, and honest lives. They also believe that those who are cruel, selfish, and immoral will be punished for their evil ways.

As a child, I had many black friends whose families experienced racism and discrimination. I was with my friend and his mother one day when a white man cursed at a black man standing nearby, using racist language. I wanted to jump on the white guy, but my friend's mother held me back, whispering: "Jesus will see him at the gates. Jesus will take care of him." Her words rang in my ears later, when I saw the racist white guy have a "come to Jesus" meeting with a local lawman, who just happened to be my grandfather, a deputy sheriff. My grandfather let this fellow know in very clear terms that his racial slurs would not be tolerated. The next time I saw him, he was converting to Christianity and repenting of his shameful behav-ior. I'm sure my friend's mother was glad to welcome him into the spiritual flock. I know that I was.

The racist's conversion to a more spiritual life and his recogni-tion that he'd been morally wrong helped confirm my childhood belief that there was justice in the world, and spirituality was the path to it. Children take comfort in that knowledge. They also need to know that there is forgiveness in this world. I noted earlier that in my forty years as a mental health professional, I've observed that the most common burdens afflicting emotional health are those related to a lack of forgiveness, and often, this is because people have not forgiven themselves.

Children need to be forgiven so that they can learn to forgive themselves. I can't tell you how many adults I have counseled who were haunted by things they did in their childhoods that went unforgiven—a broken heirloom, an unkind remark, an injury inflicted. So many people walk around blaming themselves for issues over which they have no control. Some never forgive themselves for being victims, which is an incredible tragedy.

Parents need to forgive their children. If punishment is in order, then mete it out, forgive, and move on. And make certain the child knows that all is forgiven. Don't saddle your child with the sort of burdens I have spent a career trying to lift from the backs of deeply hurt and emotionally troubled men and women. Children should be taught that a path to forgiveness is open to them. If a child does wrong, don't make her wait days or weeks for punishment and forgiveness. Lift the burden as quickly as possible. Otherwise, the child will punish herself, perhaps for a lifetime. Believe me, I've seen it happen. Often, children are tougher on themselves than their parents would ever be, and the lack of forgiveness can trigger serious long-term mental health issues.

There are spiritual paths to forgiveness available to children and adults. Many faiths practice forgiveness through prayer, confession, redemption through good deeds, and, of course, baptism. When children express interest in spirituality, it is often because of those paths to forgiveness and their appeal. The more you can teach these pathways, the more your child will understand and accept her failings—and yours too.

MAKING A DIFFERENCE

Children learn very early in their lives that they depend on others for survival. Most don't develop a sense of their own identities until around the age of two, according to research. By the age of four, children begin to ponder why they exist, or what their purpose is. While this is a question long pondered in depth by intellectuals as "man's search for meaning," children express it in simpler spiritual terms: "Why did God (or the supreme being of choice) make me?"

Children reach a point where they want to believe that there is something special about them, to give meaning to their lives. This is a path to self-love and self-worth, and to a sense of purpose, which gives a child not only inner strength but the sense that they have a contribution to make. When I began playing football for the University of North Texas, I was exposed for the first time to other athletes who felt their abilities were a spiritual blessing. When they thanked God before and after a game, they were dead serious. Today, I have friends who are or were professional football players, and many of them also believe that God is the source of their athletic prowess. A great number of athletes believe that God works through them and their talents. It is their own way of feeling blessed and unique.

Children express their spirituality when they sense that there is a greater power at work in their lives than themselves or even their parents. When your child shares those feelings with you, be supportive and encouraging of their spiritual development.

THE QUEST FOR INFINITE WISDOM

When children feel threatened or stressed, it gives them a sense of security to believe that there is a source of strength and wisdom available to them. We all can benefit from having faith in a higher power. My patient Nicky was nine years old when she experienced every child's worst fear—separation from her parents in a traumatic experience. The subway train doors closed before she could follow her parents into their car, and they were separated. The train took off, leaving her alone in the station. She was frightened, and then when two men approached her, she became terrified. They said they would protect her, but they grabbed her and began tearing at her clothing. She prayed to God as they attacked her.

She told me that as she prayed, a bright light appeared and frightened the men. Then there was a loud sound like a thunderclap. The men ran. A soothing wave swept over her. She felt safe. Within a few minutes her parents returned to the station. At first they were tearful and apologetic and relieved, but then they were stunned by her calm self-confidence and serene presence.

Nicky told her parents what had happened. They were angry and alarmed that she was attacked, but then they expressed skepticism about her account of what had happened. They theorized that maybe a police officer had shone a flashlight or fired a warning shot to frighten the attackers off. But when Nicky told me the story, she had no doubt that God had intervened, and she told me that she planned to repay God by serving as a missionary.

Another patient, David, twelve, offered a similar story that occurred when he was six. He reported that he was awakened by a storm. He looked out the window and saw a funnel cloud from a tornado in the distance. He was frozen with fear. His parents were asleep at the other end of the house. Unable to move, David prayed instead. He did not ask God to save him, but to save his parents.

Suddenly a voice told him to move away from the window, he said. He looked around, but no one was there. A second time the voice commanded him to move, this time louder. Again, he could find no source for the voice. When the warning came a third time, he obeyed, leaping off the bed and falling to the floor. Just then, a large board came flying through the window and hit the bed where he had been sleeping. It was clear that David would have been killed if he had stayed in bed. His parents and others were skeptical of his story about the voice, but David stuck to it, and who could blame him?

FULFILLING SPIRITUAL NEEDS

Many people have personal stories of "miracles" produced by what they believed to be spiritual sources. One of my favorites is the story of the staircase of the Loretto Chapel in Santa Fe, New Mexico. About a hundred years ago, the Sisters of Loretto built a school and chapel designed in the same style as the Sainte-Chapelle in Paris. When they finished the chapel, they were astonished that there was no room to build a stairway to the loft. Many carpenters were called upon, but they all shook their heads, saying a stairway required much more space than was available. They suggested two alternatives; use a ladder, or tear the whole thing down and start over. But the sisters, being women of God, were not discouraged. They called upon Saint Joseph by starting a ten-day novena, but on the ninth day a gray-haired man, carrying only a toolbox, appeared on a donkey, and asked if he could build the staircase. The sisters, ecstatic and grateful, gave him permission.

Inside the old man's toolbox were a hammer, a saw, and a T-square. It took him eight months to build the staircase, using no nails and no center support. He did it in a very small space, making two complete 360-degree turns with perfect curves. He used pegs to hold the thirty-three steps together. The carpenter disappeared before the sisters could offer to pay him.

When they inquired about him at the lumber company, there was no record of his purchases. The staircase still stands, as does the mystery of the humble carpenter on the donkey.

LOVE CONQUERS DEATH

Children begin to grasp the finality of death as the end of life on earth, and the possibility of an afterlife, around the age of five. Up to that point, they often believe that the deceased may return at some point, resulting in questions such as: "Where did she go?" "Is she coming back?"

As children learn of the possibility of life after death in the spiritual world, they naturally have questions about the nature of that existence and the form the soul or spirit takes. It can be a challenge to provide answers other than as matters of faith, since we don't have a lot of testimony from "the other side." It just so happens that I'm one of the few to have "died" and come back to tell about the experience. In 1995, I had a heart attack. Medics at first could detect no heartbeat, and my family was informed that I was on my way to the hereafter. But the medics refused to give up, and within a few minutes, they managed to get my old ticker ticking again.

I came back with some memories of where I'd been. I felt this wonderful sensation that I can only describe as a "sweetness," along with this notion that all things were understandable. I also felt surrounded by love. For whatever reason, I returned to this world, either because of the dedication of my medics or the determination of a higher authority that my earthly mission was incomplete. Like others who've started to "cross over" but returned, I experienced a twinge of disappointment that my journey to the hereafter had been delayed. I also returned with a much stronger spiritual side.

Whatever your personal beliefs in matters of the spirit and the afterlife, it is your duty as a parent to give your child guidance and a foundation for dealing with the inevitability of death and, especially, the grief of losing a loved one. Grief is a powerful and potentially debilitating emotion. When children lose a grandparent or even a pet, they need coping mechanisms, just as we all do.

Sixty percent of adults who lose a mate die within two years, according to research. The loss of a loved one produces some of the highest stress levels experienced in a lifetime, and health challenges often result within six weeks. Children are often frightened as well as stressed because they are confronted with the possibility that "if Grandma can die, so can I."

It helps children and adults to understand that grief is a natural process for coping with trauma. You can help your child by noting that the feelings that accompany grief are very common and even healthy, and that it is okay to express them. Also assure her that, over time, the sadness will diminish. We grieve no matter what we believe about the afterlife and no matter what religious beliefs we subscribe to. It is a reaction to loss. Yet spiritual beliefs can be comforting in times of grief, and your child may benefit from spiritual guidance.

The majority of Americans believe in an afterlife in some form, and there has been research showing that such beliefs can have physical and emotional benefits. It is also helpful for children to focus on honoring the life of the individual who has died by remembering good things accomplished, and shared moments of happiness. If there was a long illness or pain, it can also benefit the child to talk about the relief from suffering that death has provided. Most important, honor the person and note that the child's memories of the person will live on.

THE PLAN

Most children have the spiritual perception that each of us is held accountable one day. This concept, which is found in most faiths, is that evil is punished and goodness is rewarded. I would suggest some specific exercises to convey this article of faith, and help your child grasp the concept.

Day 1

Discuss a real event or incident in which there appears to be an injustice, such as Hurricane Katrina or a bombing that killed innocents in Iraq. Talk about the fact that justice might be served in ways that are beyond our grasp. (Example: God will smile on the storm victims and punish the bombers. Or karma might happen.) Also discuss how forgiveness might play a role for the victim(s) and the person committing the offense.

Day 2

Discuss the "Serenity Prayer":

> God grant me the serenity
> to accept the things I cannot change;
> courage to change the things I can;
> and the wisdom to know the difference.

Consider that this prayer offers methods for dealing with injustice and practicing forgiveness. How does this prayer offer empowerment to individuals?

Day 3

Discuss the Golden Rule—*Do unto others as you would have them do unto you*—and how it relates to justice. What behaviors do you consider fair and just? Come up with examples of how you and your child can treat others fairly. Discuss situations in which you treated someone unjustly, and how you might do it differently.

Day 4: "Specialness" Spirituality Needs

- Talk about the special talents and abilities of your child and other family members, and how those gifts can be used to benefit others.
- Review the spiritual lives of famous people who might inspire your child.
- Have your child create a story about using her talents to achieve greatness. Talk about the pitfalls and temptations that might be encountered, and the ultimate, spiritual awards of using your gifts for the greater good.

Day 5: Grief and Loss

Share your thoughts on death and the afterlife with your child when someone close to you dies. Explain that there are many beliefs and concepts related to life after death. Ask your child what he thinks about it.

- Take your child to a funeral of someone not close to them so that they can witness the rituals without grief or strong emotional attachment. Explain the burial process, and what those grieving are going through.
- Have your spiritual leader, such as a pastor or rabbi, discuss your faith with your child, as well as other beliefs and how they compare.

LIFE'S GREAT MYSTERIES

No matter what the parents' beliefs are, children need spiritual guidance to answer their inevitable questions and curiosities. It is entirely natural that they express interest in and connections to spiritual concepts. Be prepared, and rest assured that sometimes there are no right or wrong answers. Sometimes the answers may lie beyond human understanding—but it is helpful for your children to hear your beliefs too. Children need to understand that they are part of the universal community—something greater than themselves. They have a basic human need to be loved, to belong, and to seek answers to the age-old questions. Who knows? With your help, your child may grow up to provide humankind with answers about the meaning of life and the existence of an afterlife.

Epilogue

The human spirit has incredible self-healing powers. I have seen people rally and recover from illnesses and disabilities that were thought to be insurmountable. These individuals have no super-powers. They've made no pact with either God or the devil. But somehow, they've tapped into a source of power and strength that lies within each of us. I believe that men, women, and children have abilities for physical, emotional, and mental healing and regenera-tion that we have yet to comprehend, let alone master.

We all face challenges. That is part of life. Maintaining physical, emotional, and mental balance is a daily challenge for most of us. Even great wisdom, emotional strength, and physical courage do not keep those challenges from coming at us day to day. We should welcome them as opportunities for learning and growth, even at my advanced age. Not long ago, I challenged my daughter's answer to a math problem, and she insisted—rudely, I thought—that she was right and I was wrong.

"Dad, you have always told me to speak the truth, and I am doing that. Why are you getting so angry with me?"

I had to admit to myself that my desire to be right might have been over the top. Still, I have a mathematics degree. I had to be right. My daughter challenged me to put my ego aside and look for truth. As it turned out, the kid had the right answer. Mr. Mathematics Degree was wrong.

Our children need our guidance. They need our support, our love, and our understanding. But most of all, they need us to listen to them with clear minds, because they have things to teach us too. After all, it will most likely be one of our children who offers the next solution to one of life's great mysteries.

FRESH MIND

From the age of two, we envision and build our world, weaving it according to our perceptions. This self-constructed view becomes our window on the world. When something happens that runs contrary to our view, we falter and rebel against it like spoiled children denied a pacifier. This childish rage will continue unabated unless we accept a more mature view of existence—one that does not feature all of the planets rotating around us.

Our capacity to love and generate love grows in direct correlation to our willingness to expand our view of existence and to understand that each individual is just one element of something much greater. Parents are given that gift when children enter their lives. It is our duty to share the gift of love and understanding with them. We must commit to this mission, and keep growing ourselves. Every day we are required to open ourselves to the eternal and universal flame of love.

THE MANY DIMENSIONS OF LOVE

In the beginning of this book I assured you that when you concluded the program, you would have the tools to create a loving bond between you and your child. You now have the tools to accomplish these goals, at least from the outside in. But there are essential requirements for building them from the inside out. As often happens, you'll find it best put in the Bible: "If I speak in the tongues of men and of angels, but have not love, I am only a resounding gong or a clanging cymbal" (I Corinthians 13:1–3).

Consider what you have learned in this book as the beginning of a path rather than a complete journey. Your path to loving and being loved by your child will change course from time to time. Your relationship will change over the years, and hopefully, it will grow richer and deeper as your love for each other is strengthened through understanding and forgiveness. There are as many definitions of love as there are people and experiences. I've identified at least seven different dimensions of relationship love. The most profound is spiritual love, or *agape*, which is defined as unconditional love based on inner goodness. The Christian God is purported to love humankind in this manner because of the spirit within each person. Lasting bonds of unconditional love should be the goal of every parent and every child, because it is given without judgment and maintained through forgiveness.

Philos is another dimension of love, that of a loving friendship. This type of love is based on a commitment and loyalty to one another. This powerful connection features mutual reliance and withstands many trials. A similar dimension is called *storage* love, a love that develops over time through trust based on consistency.

Perhaps one of the most confusing forms is *pragma* love. This is a *pragmatic* form, based on a logical relationship between two people who have similar goals and passions for accomplishment. There is a unifying set of accepted behaviors and expectations that support such a love. For example, when two people are excited about discovering a scientific breakthrough or work together to win honors, their journey toward shared goals builds a *pragma* relationship based on mutual expectations. Being in the same family invites this kind of love.

There is a similar form of love based on shared behaviors, called *mania* love. This is marked by a sense of possession and pride in the relationship. The relationship is carefully guarded, and outsiders are not welcomed. Think of a mother hen protecting her chicks and defending them beyond rationality. Obviously, if this is taken to extreme, it can become smothering.

The love dimension that most people identify as "the love connection" is referred to as the *eros* dimension, which features passion, sensuality, and eroticism. This is most often expressed in romantic involvement between two people devoted to each other, whether in marriage or some other form of long-term commitment. However, eros can also be at play in a passionate affair or a short-term relationship. This dimension does not require a sexual focus; it can also be expressed in a mutual passion for expression and imagination. In fact, adults who fall in love at this level often become childlike. Yet another form, *ludos* love, may actually be more of a predecessor to a loving relationship, because it involves one person soliciting the love of another. Flirting is a good example. But even a smile of support or a gentle touch on the shoulder can be defined within this dimension.

As we mature, these different forms of love may blend together in varying combinations. Dimensions of love are easily misunderstood and can create tension, but some loves are more complicated than others. Each of us has unique approaches and varying capacities to express and receive love. Those individual differences can result in misunderstandings, confusion, and hurt feelings.

John was a very precocious eight-year-old when I first saw him. He was hyperactive and disrespectful, and this stemmed from his fear of losing the attention of his parents. The firstborn of six children, John had gotten used to being the center of attention as a baby, but then all these brothers and sisters began arriving, and he felt neglected. My treatment approach was not complicated. We worked with his parents, helping them give John more loving attention through some of the techniques mentioned in the book.

John wasn't a tough case to treat, but his behavior problems exemplify how complex the parent-child bonds can become. This bright and sensitive boy remained a patient throughout his childhood, and I witnessed him go through nearly every dimension of a loving relationship. Initially, he needed ludos love because he was so frightened and needy. The parents focused on John to fulfill that need, but it still took some coaching and training for him to realize that his parents could love each of their children equally.

Once John got with the program, he settled into a pragma form of loving acceptance as a member of a large family. During his early teen years, he underwent the typical search for identity and independence. He rebelled a bit, but then found direction in the martial arts, which allowed him to channel his energies in a positive direction. His parents responded by adapting with an agape form of love, giving him some slack with their unconditional, nonjudgmental affection.

John eventually became a Golden Gloves champion and a coach, but most important, he and his parents built lasting, loving bonds. Their relationship demonstrates that if you want a lasting love relationship with your child, you must be prepared to accept and give love in all of its forms. Your love for your child will shift, but it should not dissipate. This mixture of cross-communications can be a source of strength, and even evidence of maturation between parent and child. In many cultures these various stages of love are honored through rituals and pronouncements.

It may be hard to honor the changes in love relationships, because the older ones are comforting and traditional. But parents have to accept this as part of the deal. Their bonds should grow stronger over the years, but it will take patience, perseverance, and courage.

SELF-LOVE

It is said that a person cannot love another more than he can love himself. I would probably edit that to say that we receive only as much as we are capable of giving—and that can limit some people terribly.

When I was researching the elements of healthy, therapeutic relationships at the University of Arkansas Rehabilitation Center, I became intrigued by one particular feature—*unconditional positive regard*. This is a measure of how much someone cares for a person without regard to the person's behavior. I developed a measure that consisted of six levels.

The first level was the least regard for the person, with the highest amount of prejudice. It would be like walking into a situation where you were doomed from the beginning because of conditions surrounding you. The highest level occurred when a person won high regard even if he was rude or disrespectful.

The scale looked like that on page 273.

This research was designed to help us understand how people feel about being interviewed in therapy. We called this dimension the "love connection," because it revolved around the concept of agape love. As expected, the people who responded best to the relationship correlated highly with this scale, that is, to the first five levels. What we learned was that most individuals are not comfortable being in the presence of a totally unconditional loving situa-

Empathy Scale

Levels of Empathy

People felt supported and cared for best at these levels.

However, people became suspicious when regard was freely given.

| No regard | Regard only minimally | Regard given under high conditions | Regard given with low conditions | Regard easily with few conditions | Total regard |

tion. They didn't trust it. Without some method for earning high regard, they became paranoid.

Individuals say they want total love from another. They want the freedom of knowing that regardless of what they do or say, they will be loved unconditionally, as a parent loves a child. I have heard so many criminals say, "My momma loves me anyway. She has to. She's my momma."

I have no doubt that most mothers love their children regardless of the pain they cause or the number of lives they wreck through their selfishness. If Mrs. Manson and Mrs. Hitler loved their sons, well, good for them. I suppose I will love my children even if they ruin me and get me thrown into prison.

The answer to the riddle of unconditional love is not how it affects the child or another person, but how it affects you, the sender. The research does show some influence from the power of extended love, but the biggest receiver is the person offering it. There is a boomerang effect. The passion of love can heal from within. The more you put out without ego or selfishness, the more healing you do to your soul.

In times of high stress (and there will always be some when you are a parent), your best weapon is a double-ought load of un-conditional love. When your child is rebelling, mouthing off, and otherwise infuriating you, lock and load the unconditional love. Practice being a grown-up. Do not let the child dictate your re-sponse. Reframe with a long-range view, and disarm the child with love.

That is the central message of this book. Your child needs you to be the grown-up. Isaac Newton formulated many laws of physics. One of his major contributions was to show the influence of one body's gravity on another. Although his conclusions have been taught in every physics class in the world, he never could formulate exact measurements of more than two bodies on each other. Imag-ine how little we know about the influence of love.

THE PHYSICS OF LOVE

Love is invisible, but so are atoms and electrons. Even so, atoms and electrons are subject to mathematical models, and there are meth-ods for predicting their behavior. But there are no mathematical models for measuring love. Still, I've devised a system to predict lov-ing behavior. It consists of three laws of love:

- Love can be created and enhanced by both success and failure.
- Love is omnidirectional, meaning that it affects everything.
- Love is the glue of life.

Love Can Be Created and Enhanced by Both Success and Failure

This phenomenon is an amazing feature of this powerful force. If you attempt to reinforce it, it will grow. If you attempt to express love, and it is rejected, the seeds will eventually grow. A touch, a good word, even a smile, will bring some particle of love to life. Never withhold your love.

Love Is Omnidirectional, Meaning That It Affects Everything

Both receiver and producer create love within themselves. It influences everything from cell production to muscle strength, brainpower, and every element of the body. It is infectious and unavoidable.

Love Is the Glue of Life

A professor once posed this situation: If the nucleus of an atom is the size of an orange, the distance to the nearest electron circling it would be longer than a football field. A student asked the professor what would keep the electrons hanging together. The professor responded: "Love." Maybe he was right. All the electrons stay together because of their love for one another.

FINAL NOTE

I have always been a dog lover, and I think the greatest compliment would be to be told that I could love like my dog loved me. There was Pal, who protected me against harm with his ferocious bark and growl, and Yoshi, who walked me into health from my heart attack. My dog now is called Patches, because I found him in a ditch and he has no recognizable bloodline. He is a patchwork of genetics, and probably the smartest dog in the world.

I mention dogs not merely to express my love of them, but to confide to you that I believe that many dogs may really be angels. I believe this is so because they express love the way I believe our souls are meant to. They are loyal, and unless they are mistreated, they will always greet you with joy and love. They forgive you for your misbehavior with a petting or a scratch. And they always like to listen to your troubles or songs—even my bad poetry.

Don't you wonder why we can't love each other like that?

Resources

Bartels, Andreas and Semir Zeki. "The Neural Correlates of Maternal and Romantic Love." *NeuroImage* 21 (2004): 1155–1166.

Berk, Laura. *Infants and Children,* 5th edition. New York: Pearson, 2005.

———. *Infants, Children and Adolescents,* 5th edition. New York: Pearson, 2005.

Bower, Bruce. "Violent Developments." *Science News* 169, no. 21, pp. 328–329.

Bradbury, Andrew, *Develop Your NLP Skills,* 3rd edition. Philadelphia: Kogan Page, 2006.

Brown, Jason. *Mind, Brain, and Consciousness.* New York: Academic Press, 1977.

Burgoon, Judee and Thomas Salne. *The Unspoken Dialogue.* Boston: Houghton Mifflin, 1978.

Dreikeurs, Rudolf. *Children: The Challenge.* New York: Plume, 1964.

Levine, Madeline. *The Price of Privilege.* New York: HarperCollins, 2006.

Loges, Shirley, ed. "Chemical Abuse and IQ." *Mensa Research Journal* 37, no. 2 (Summer 2006).

Moss, Erin and Dobson Moss. "The Place of Spirituality." *The Register Report* (Council for the National Register of Health Service Providers in Psychology), Spring 2007, 10–19.

Myers, David. *Social Psychology.* New York: McGraw-Hill, 2002.

Obrzut, John and George Hynd. *Child Neuropsychology.* New York: Academic Press, 1986.

Rosa, Emily. "A Close Look at Therapeutic Touch." *The Journal of the American Medical Association* 279, no. 13 (April 1998).

Sabbagh, Leslie. "The Teen Brain, Hard at Work." *Scientific American Mind,* August 2006, 21–23.

Segterstrale, Ullica and Peter Molnar. *Nonverbal Communication: Where Nature Meets Culture.* Mahwah, N.J.: Lawrence Erlbaum, 1997.

Siegel, Daniel. *The Developing Mind.* New York: Guilford, 1999.

Sigelman, Carol and Elizabeth Rider. *Life-Span Human Development,* 5th edition. New York: Thomson, 2006.

Vasta, Ross, Marshall Haith, Scott Miller. *Child Psychology,* 3rd edition. New York: John Wiley, 1999.

Watson, Lyall. *Dark Nature.* New York: HarperPerennial, 1995.

Index